I0521583

The
Elven-Faerie
Grimoire

# POCKET EDITION

Published from
The Joshua Free Imprint – JFI Publications
Mardukite Borsippa HQ, San Luis Valley, Colorado
Founding Church of Mardukite Zuism,
Mardukite Academy & Systemology Society
*for religious and educational purposes only.*

# The

# Elven Faerie

# Grimoire

## A DRUID'S BOOK OF SHADOWS, LIGHT & ENCHANTMENT

Based on the work by Joshua Free
Edited by Rowen Gardner

## THE JOSHUA FREE IMPRINT
### JFI PUBLICATIONS

© 2023, JOSHUA FREE

ISBN : 979-8-9871249-8-7

ELVENOMICON SERIES-I BOOK-2

Premiere Pocket Paperback Edition — *May 2023*

*Mardukite Druidism (Grade-I, D-Series)*

**mardukite.com**

## You Are Called To Live a Magical Life!

Reclaim the Enchantment of the Old Ways!
Practice mystical Druidic rites from a complete
"Book of Shadows" that has inspired hundreds
of esoteric magick traditions and "New Age"
publications from the underground for decades!

Open the door to ancient mysteries of magic!
Now you can easily and safely explore
rituals and ceremonies inspiring Faery Wicca
and American revivals of Celtic Witchcraft
with a new approach to such things as
casting circles, self-initiations and the sabbats.

Solitary and group practitioners alike will find
"The Elven-Faerie Grimoire"
is a handbook worth its weight in gold!

Joshua Free has been paving the way through
the esoteric foliage of nature magick for
over 25 years, and presents this revised portion
of the original "Elvenomicon" volume as
a stand-alone pocket guide for the first time!

"The Elven-Faerie Grimoire" is your invitation
to participate in celebrating a magical life
in the Celtic-Druid and Elven-Faerie traditions.

If you want the best guide possible as your
companion for your annual journey through
the seasonal Wheel of the Year, then
"The Elven-Faerie Grimoire" by Joshua Free
is the ideal practical manual for you.

Titles in the forthcoming
2023 pocket paperback series
based on the "*Elvenomicon*"
by Joshua Free

Elvenomicon Series-I

*The Secret Book of Elven-Faerie*

*The Elven-Faerie Grimoire*

*The Enchanted Forest*

Elvenomicon Series-II

*Secret Legacy of Elves & Faeries*

*The Elven-Faerie Spellbook*

*The Book of Ogham*

Series titles coming soon
from JFI Publications

# TABLET OF CONTENTS

## INTRODUCTION

*by Joshua Free*

My participation in the legacy behind *"The Elven-Faerie Grimoire"* began during the mid-1990's in the midst of a critical resurgence of 'New Age' revival—and foremost among these popular interests: the *Celts* and *Druids.*

*Elven-Faerie Grimoire* is an integral part of a greater body of work pertaining to my own personal involvement with *Elven-Faerie* traditions of Druidism for over 25 years. This material was imparted to me by direct personal 'apprenticeship' with its modern developers and this is reflected in what I've presented as the first *Elvenomicon* series.

The original *"Elvenomicon"* series—a trilogy in one volume—first circulated in the underground as *"The Book of Elven-Faerie,"* but I later renamed as *Elvenomicon* to avoid confusing the total collection of work with the title of the first discourse it contained: *Book of Elven-Faerie*—retitled *Secret Book of Elven-Faerie* for this present series reissue. It is a separate volume from the other two parts in the trilogy: *Greenwood Forest Grimoire* and

*The Elven-Faerie Grimoire*—the first one being retitled for this series as *Enchanted Forest*. Collectively, this original trilogy comprises *Elvenomicon* 'Series-1' and its contents is my own personal presentation of Elven-Faerie Druidic Tradition for the past *20* years.

The subject of 'Faery-Faith in Celtic Countries' frequently occupies the attention of Druids throughout the ages, but also practitioners of modern Elven-Faerie magical traditions. The influence on 'New Age' revivals of 'Faery Wicca' and 'Celtic Witchcraft' are equally significant. Many customs and 'sabbats' observed today—and quite often taken for granted—very much owe their foundations to the ancient 'Celtic-Faerie Tradition' and what is better known as *"Druidism."*

The *Elvenomicon* series is the result of many years of experimentation, deliberation and contemplation spent in personal dedication to the Elven Tradition before attempting to set this version of it in down in print. It is derived from deep underground sources—ones that has never been revealed by any of its initiates, but which is frequently drawn from by the same—as obvious by compositions of many popular New Age titles that emerged during the 1990's—and which provided many of the original New Age "covens," "groups" and "groves" with inspiration to outline a "*Book of Shadows, Light & Enchantment*" independent of traditional 'New Age' Wiccan manuals influenced by Gerald Gardner, Aleister Crowley, The Key of Solomon, Charles Leland and/or Margaret Murray (and so forth).

Until a blatant presence of published Elven-Faerie and Druid Traditions in 1990's esoteric occultism, there were very few readily available alternatives to the "traditional witchcraft" scene for neopagan revivals. It is evident by iconic resurgences of "elven," "druidic," "dragon" and "faerie" motifs in culture that this other covert underground movement of increasing human awareness has proven, in part, quite effective.

The Elven Way and Faerie Tradition are now a part of nearly all relevant 21st century 'new consciousness', 'new thought' or otherwise earth-oriented forms of "nature mysticism." As such, *this* work—as a "*living grimoire*"—has been reevaluated and revised several times before arriving in its currently refined state. And this happens frequently when one is working to solidify the Elven "words of light" to the printed page—for they are fluid and dynamic, shimmering etherically in the waves of a cosmic sea.

Only Druidry and indigenous shamanism reflect the same type of spiritual "pathway" for Human Ascension that is alluded to in Elven Tradition. And if supplemented with our latest spiritual developments for "Systemology," an Elven-Faerie Druid Tradition can be an effective stepping stone on this greater Pathway.

Although most New Age texts equate Elves and other elemental faerie beings exclusively with the Otherworld or Astral Plane, more experienced practitioners understand the connection between these races and a "very real" legacy of Elven-Dragon traditions and the *Tuatha d'Anu* migrating westward across Europe from Mesopotamia and Anatolia, carrying with them a vast tradition and repository of knowledge from the "Ancient Mystery School." These matters are discussed at length in my previous discourse for this series, *"Book of Elven-Faerie"* or rather, *'The Secret Book of Elven-Faerie'*.

The term "Elven magic" ("Elven magick") is used to distinguish this "Elven-Ffayrie" system—also called the *"Edaphic Tradition"*—from others in the 'New Age'. However, to the Elves themselves, magic is simply "magic" and it comes from an innate faculty—not some "supernatural" facet of life or intellectual study. Once again: Magic is *not* a "supernatural" power. On the contrary, magick is quite "natural" and, in this universe, follows principles of "natural law" or "cosmic law" even if not commonly understood.

When Humans refer to "magick," they are simply referring to an esoteric study and creative use of forces in the Universe—the same principles that manifest reality on a moment-to-moment basis. It is the practical application of the true knowledge and lore in everyday life. It should always be enacted *towards* one's own Ascension and in acts to manifest a harmonious world for all Life.

True "magick" in the Elven Tradition is innate—they do not require years of study

14

and training that the Wizard Schools of Humans and "Fey-Touched" must resort to. The Elven-Ffayrie simply do not see "magick" as something "outside" of themselves. It is developed and refined as part of their everyday natural life—over a period of progressive self-discovery, just as a Human might choose to refine their own personal tastes and skills, affecting muscle memory or some other artificial automaticity for experiencing (and creating) reality.

Wisdom of experience—and I mean Self-Honest experiences from a point of true actualized Awareness—develops with time, and this is something that Elven-Ffayrie races are not short on while residing in the 'Lands Beyond'. Elves and faerie folk also view magick as a part of art. When something created or changed becomes charged or imbued with energy as a result of intention, it becomes art—and they learned to use this art to shape the natural world that we see all around us—our "reality." And magick—in all of its forms—will create, transform or even destroy some reflection of our global "reality."

"Magickal feats"—as conceived and purported by Humans—are accomplished via the activation of the mind's subconscious faculties—which becomes "potential power." It may be activated with specific use of symbolism and imagery or focal aids that help an individual direct or channel energy. We are always actively participating in this *game*—but it is only with our *conscious* participation that we have the power to create.

Many customs and methods of raising energy for this very purpose exist—ritual movements, breathing exercises, ceremonial dances—all of which entice the awareness of the total *Self* to become actively involved in bringing about desired results. All intentional acts are "magical"—even when it is cyclic self-talk of defeatism—and we put our awareness and attention-energies into wherever our focus lies.

All acts, whether mundane or esoteric—are magical when they are movements of energy that create change—in accordance with true will—and following natural laws and cosmic principles that may or may not be widely understood. The Human Condition is easily distracted, and so rituals and ceremonial drama; use of music and vocalized intentions; alternative attire and altar dressings; fragrance of sweet and musty incense and flickering firelight—all are effectively used to bring the *Self* into full awareness and control of the *Self* alone.

It is important to realize—especially if you desire a true understanding of "Elven magick"—that it is not the rituals and incantations themselves that hold the "power" in magic. A catalyst only represents potential until properly used—and that use is based on ability. "Magickal abilities" come from within—first and foremost—from the part of the "individual" that is not "separated" from the All—but is interconnected and linked absolutely to the fundamental Oneness of reality.

Elven-Druid Wizards and Mystics channel energy currents tied to Elemental Forces. When present in ceremony, these energies are considered external "higher powers." They are called by "will"—but often they are simply energetically attracted to the use of the magic conducted naturally. Since we know they are always present, the Wizard or Druid uses a form of long-standing etiquette when calling and dismissing any external—or thought-formed—energies and entities.

"*Elven-Faerie Grimoire*" provides a practical application of Elven-Faerie lore and Druidic magic—as does its companion volume, "*The Elven-Faerie Grimoire*"—that has stood the test of time now for over decades and which will continue to inspire aligned realizations of the Elven Way in perpetuity.

—Joshua Free, Spring Equinox 2023
Borsippa HQ, San Luis Valley

# THE
# ELVEN-FAERIE
# GRIMOIRE

# elements of tradition and the elven way

Elven-Faerie tradition alludes to a singular unifying Oneness—an ALL interconnected with All life and energy in the Cosmos. However, the energy that manifests the world of forms that we experience within the parameters of physical reality (within a Human sensory range) is filtered down and condensed into a series of perceived 'levels' or 'degrees', 'vibrations' and 'frequencies' which are constantly in motion in accord with the Cosmic Law of ALL.

There are—in reality—no actual separations between these varying degrees although we experience them that way subjectively as individuals perceiving a "world around us"—not always realizing that it is *us* that projects the separation of "things" from other "things." This holistic type of "*systemology*" is "meta-thinking" for most Humans. Some elemental schema that follow in this chapter-lesson do relate directly to traditional more familiar Fourfold Elemental paradigms aligned to *Tuatha d'Anu* lore.

However, Elven-Ffayrie traditions often record their Elemental schema in other methods that are not restricted to cross-quarter symmetry many *Seekers* have undoubtedly encountered in other sources of western magical tradition. They more commonly appear as threefold, sixfold and even ninefold "aspects" or "elements"—called "*duile*" in Celtic fae traditions.

Neodruids and other New Age Wizards have also called the same: "*aires*"—so named after the "Four Winds." Sometimes the classification of elements are misunderstood—for example, because "*Nwyvre*" may be interpreted as both "*Akasha*" and "*Fire*," but as you will see, Elvish Wizards interpret the traditional "Fire Element" a bit differently when experienced in the "Otherworld."

THE THREEFOLD ELEMENTAL SCHEMA

Element of Land: bone, tissue, muscle, skin, soil, ground, minerals, crystals, plant life, vegetation, and mainland ecosystem.

<u>Element of Sky</u>: oxygen, lungs, voice, circulatory system, winds, upper atmosphere, clouds, vapor, and winged life.

<u>Element of Sea</u>: blood, fluids, hormones, neurochemicals, natural bodies of water, running water and marine life.

THE SIXFOLD ELEMENTAL SCHEMA

<u>Element of Stone</u>: "brown magick"—animals, business, gems, metals and soil.

<u>Element of Earth</u>: "green magick"—agriculture, ecology, fertility, forests, herbalism and trees.

<u>Element of Vapor & Cloud</u>: "indigo magick"—quantum physics, Otherworld magick, psychic powers, spirits and time travel.

<u>Element of Wind</u>: "yellow magick"—alertness, books, communication, con-

fidence, knowledge, study, reading and writing.

<u>Element of Sun</u>: "red magick" & "orange magick"—alchemy, art, courage, healing, love, passion, strength, success and attraction.

<u>Element of Sea</u>: "blue magick"—creativity, dreams, love, emotion, glamour, the moon, enchantment, mysticism, peace, tranquility, understanding and visions.

## THE NINEFOLD ELEMENTAL SCHEMA

<u>Element of Salt</u>—Land: nighttime, northwest, white, consecration ceremonies and purification.

<u>Element of Earth</u>—Land: midnight, north, green, trees/forest growth magick and fertility.

<u>Element of Stone</u>—Land: evening, northeast, brown, crystal magick, charging and protection.

<u>Element of Wind</u>—Sky: morning twilight, east, yellow, new beginnings, insight and summoning.

<u>Element of Star(fire)</u>—Sky: dawn, southeast, white, dreams, wish magick and awareness.

<u>Element of Sun</u>—Sky: noon, south, gold, insight, willpower, strength and leadership.

<u>Element of Vapor & Cloud</u>—Sea: twilight, southwest, astral magick, Otherworld work and enchantments.

<u>Element of Sea</u>—Sea: sunset, west, blue, subconscious magick, dreams, healing and love.

<u>Element of Rain</u>—Sea: dust, west-northwest, purple, emotions, emotional healing, cleansing, love and beauty.

Practice of Elemental Magick in Elvish Wizardry is typically composed of three main levels of progression—or degrees of experience. They relate not only to the development of one's abilities, but are also the same steps taken for ritualized exercises in meditation for effective physical magick:—

1. Dedication: study and initiation.
2. Purification: grounding and creating sacred space.
3. Invocation: calling forth and dismissing Elementals.

When utilizing rites of "Elemental Magick," a Wizard gains astral, spiritual and subconscious experience with a specific element. While all normal ritual observations will employ the four Elemental Quarters of the Middle World, Elvish Wizards often focus on a single element during personal meditations—working intensely with a particular aspect of the Elemental Kingdoms.

By encountering each single element individually, an Apprentice Wizard to gains experience and "authority" with a each specific element before calling its powers directly in a ceremonial/ritual setting. However, when an affinity to a particular element emerges be warned that you will begin to assimilate attributes specific to that elemental type. For example—a Wizard who works with the Air Element most of the time may begin to develop a more *flighty*, *spacey* and *imaginative* personality. A "Fire Wizard" might develop an increased sense of personal *courage* and/or *passion*, but also *irritability* when untempered, &tc.

Elven Tradition observes four main styles or types of magickal practice. They are the ceremonial/ritualisitic (*Air*); energy and/or light work (*Fire*); use of astral or spirit vision to access the Otherworld (*Water*); and tree/forest magick (*Earth*). The "grimoires" within the current *Elvenomicon* series make a collective use of all these practices as specific to the observance of a modern "Elven-Druid Faerie Tradition."

This book does not, however, claim to substitute material of a full "magickal primer" for the novice.* In additional to elemental schema provided previously, the following are "Elemental Keys" of the four primary

---

\* For a general magick primer, see "*The Sorcerer's Handbook*" by Joshua Free (writing as Merlyn Stone in the 1990's) or the relatively more recently composed omnibus anthology *"Arcanum: The Great Magical Arcanum."*

"*duile*" as more commonly used in Elemental Magick by various Wizards, Druids and Mystics of the "Lands Above." Elsewhere in Druidic lore they are referred to as the "Elven Keys" or "Faerie Keys"—relating quite succinctly with lore introduced in a previous volume of this series regarding the "*Gifts of Faeire*"—which inspired the original Elemental "magic" correspondences of the *Tuatha D'Anu*.

---

### THE FOURFOLD ELEMENTAL SCHEMA

<u>Element of Earth</u>: Elven Key to foundation and fertility, Kingdom of Stone, North, midnight and winter, ruled by King Ghobas, pentacles and holed stones are indicative of the Stone of Fal.

<u>Element of Air</u>: Elven Key to communication and intellect, Kingdom of Wind, East, dawn and spring, ruled by King Paraldas, wands and feathers represent the Spear of Lugh.

<u>Element of Fire</u>: Elven Key to transformation and protection, Kingdom of Flame, South, noon and summer, ruled by King Djin, the blade, staff & 'golden sickle' are representations of the Sword of Nuada.

<u>Element of Water</u>: Elven Key to inner wisdom and well-being, Kingdoms of Sea, West, dusk and autumn, ruled by King Niksas, the goblet, chalice, cup, mirrors and pools follow the tradition of the Cauldron of Dagda and Kerridwen.

# casting the circle of power at the nemeton

Meditation is a common and effective practice, but there is a subconscious desire inherent in wizardry—and those called to its orders—that seeks a uniform physical ritualization or ceremony to represent energetic action of "Natural Law." For these reasons, all ritual and ceremonial observations should occur within the "Circle of Power." Here, the Elvish Wizard creates a microcosm—or fractal miniaturization—of the Universe. Currents of Elemental energy are represented in ritual with symbolic catalysts or tools.

The "Circle of Power" is really the atomic *sphere*—fractal in nature, duplicating itself in "smaller" and "larger" dimensions or degrees, "above" and "below" frequency vibrations of what Humans separate as the "physical world." It may help to envision it not as a circle, but as a multi-dimensional "sphere." In eastern traditions, the 'magic circle' is called a "mandala," but in the Elven-Druid traditions, sacred space is frequently referred to as a "*nemeton.*" This "Magick Sphere" is not only a *microcosm* of the cosmos but simultaneously a *macrocosm* —an expanded or enlarged view—of the subatomic and cellular worlds also existing "beyond" normative mortal perceptual vision. All these varying worlds or dimensions are connected in an "Absolute Reality" or unified encompassing field—what ancient Druids called "*Ceugent,*" where exists only the Source of All Being and Creation.

Preliminary ceremonial methods for a rite of casting the "Circle of Power" or "Magick Sphere" vary between known systems of practical occultism. More variations probably exist in the "New Age" concerning "Rites of the Magick Circle" than any other aspect of practical metaphysics. The "Magick Sphere" or "*Nemeton*" is a sacred place of power. It is suggested that you should bring this "magic" to the wilderness and forests—find a clearing, or if possible, a "grove of trees." There you may even call on "Earth" and "Stone" as you erect your own "stone circle" or "henge of stones."

The size of your *"kirc"* or physical "sacred circle" will vary based on the location used and the number of participants expected to be present at a given time. Understand that when you bring magick to the same place repeatedly—especially when you are permitted to leave your circle in place—the woodlands will become reminiscent of an ancient archetypal "Enchanted Forest" as the land takes on an increased "charge" over time.[*]

According to classical accounts, the *"Nemeton"* is a "sacred space" when using terminology of ancient Druids and Elves—the same vocabulary appears regarding groves and henges. One of the famous *"Drunemetons"*— a place of annual gatherings for ancient Druids, Dragon-kind and Elven-Faerie—existed somewhere in ancient Anatolia/Galatia (modern-day Turkey), revealing to us the true extent of geographic expansion once maintained by the Druids. There is even an ancient Druidic deity named as a patron of sacred space, *Nemetona*—"Goddess

---

[*] See also a later volume in this series, titled: *"The Enchanted Forest: A Druid's Grimoire of Celtic Tree Magic"* by Joshua Free.

of the Grove"—closely identifying (siimilar to 'Diana of the Forest') with a feminine form of the Dagda or Kernunnos as a male "Lord of the Forest" or Green Man. Stonehenge and Woodhenge are two basic examples in Britain of ancient structures built to mark a "*nemeton.*" Groves and henges can easily be "artificially" planted or manufactured—and consecrated to this tradition—so long as they are "left open to the sky."

The "Nemeton"—sacred space—is a critical component of practical "ritual magick" energy-work. A wizard must be free of physical, emotional and mental restraints, or bonds to the "material" degrees of existence, during "magical" operations. Creating and distinguishing "sacred space" allows both the conscious and subconscious mind to synchronize salient beliefs that "something magical is about to happen."

In the past, Druids and Elves have followed energetic vibrations or currents ("*ley lines*") of Nature to reach certain "power spots" and distinguished locations—such that even an only partially sensitive Human might describe as "enchanted" or "magical." Modern Druids, Wizards and Mystics dedicated to "green magic" continue to do this today, seeking out places for personal and overt "Earth power" to work their magick from.

A *Seeker* is encouraged to research the vibrations and energetic currents of local trees and find natural representations that reflect the stream-current or ray that best reflects your own energies and/or the function of a ritual. Additional lore to assist this is provided in the "*The Enchanted Forest*" volume within this *Elvenomicon* series. New Age practitioners frequently consider the astrophysical qualities of celestial bodies—such as the Sun and Moon—during selection of the ritual area and timing of ceremonies—especially those linked to annual seasonal cycles, such as the solstices and equinoxes.

A "*Nemeton*" for a solitary practitioner does not obviously carry the same space requirements as one intended for group (or even "coven") use. The center of the *Nemeton* is typically marked with an Altar. The same rules apply to the altar: the size and shape are dependent on your needs. Be sure to leave enough space to move around the altar within the circle without affecting *Nemeton* boundaries. For group magick—practitioners will require much more space to move around freely. Here, you might reflect on energetic tension differences between times when you are alone and when you are in a crowded room. If movement is restricted in close quarters, energy does not have the freedom to expand—and those gathered together will be more likely to draw their energies and auras *in* rather than properly project them *out*.

When you are ready to perform your magick, go to your "altar." For projective magick, it is customary to call forth and visualize a white field of light to surround yourself with—or another relevant ray-vibration of light—and ask your "Higher Self"—or interconnected consciousness—to guide and protect you in your magickal endeavors. After this, an Elvish Wizard asks for peace, grace and acknowledgment from the elemental spirits in the Universe—and then the ritual can begin:—

### CASTING THE CIRCLE OF POWER

Take a "goblet of water," holding it up to the west and say:

> *May the Spirits of Water bestow their blessing and remember.*

Take up the "bowl of salt," hold it up to the northern direction and say:

> *May the Spirits of Earth bestow their blessing and remember.*

Sprinkle a portion of the "salt" into the "water," hold it up, facing north and affirm:

> *By this alchemical expression do I transform and purify my being—consecrating my spirit to the Source of All Light and the Children of Light, the Ancient and Shinning Ones.*

Take up the "incense resin" (or stick) and hold it up to the east, saying:

> *May the Spirits of Air bestow their blessing and remember.*

Hold up the "incense burner" to the south and say:

*May the Spirits of Fire bestow their blessing and remember.*

If you are using an incense stick, light it—otherwise the coals you should be prepared within the burner. Then add some of the incense resin to it and affirm:

*By this alchemical expression do I hereby transform and purify my being, stripping away old skin, leaving my mortal body, affirming my Elven (Ffayrie) soul, consecrated to the Source of All Light and Starfire.*

Allow the incense to burn. Take the chalice of salt-water and go to the north, working clockwise around the circle, sprinkling the water lightly as you walk. Be sure to ration your use so that some remains.

Once you have moved about full circle, returning again to the north, go to your altar or 'work space' and take up the incense burner—adding some more if necessary—and go to the east, moving again around the entire boundary of the circle, slowly and deliberately. Your actions should express that you are walking or testing the boundaaries of the "ends of the Universe"—represented by the Nemeton.

Go to the north with your "magick wand,"—carrying it in your projective hand (the one you write with) and begin to inscribe your circle, tracing or defining it on a metaphysical level—where before, you were only testing and sensing it. When using a wand in this way, your projective arm usually crosses the body as you walk clockwise in your initial conjuring of the "Circle of Power."

Empower and/or envision your arm as an extension of your will, and the "magick wand" as a further extension—representing where your will meets that of the external energies that your will has summoned and attracted. See bluish-white energy projecting from your wand and imprinting the horizon of your circle at waist height. You may wish, if you are adept in visualization, to see this band of energy extending both above and below to form a "sphere."

Once you circumnavigate the "kirc," return to the central altar and address the Universe:

*Here I stand at the Entrance of the Golden Threshold. Between the Finite and Infinite Universe do I stand. The mortal spark burns deep within my being and I am flawed. The Divine spark burns deep within my being and I am flawless. Once I acknowledge the connectedness I share with the Source of All, I am complete and at one with all life in the Universe. I am a "Child of Starlight."*

Feel the presence of the "Forces of Nature" surrounding your "*Nemeton*," attracted to the "Circle of Light," that you have conjured. Acknowledge them by calling out:

*I feel many varieties of energy imbued with Light and Life from the Otherworld coming to the edge of my Circle of Power. I hereby invite you in, all friendly spirits who aid in the positive magick of Nature. Witness and defend my ritual. Shield and protect this Sacred Nemeton, the Holy Mandala consecrated to the Light, the Children of Light, the Ancient and Shinning Ones. Being a Child of Starlight, I stand here to recognize and honor my ancestors and preserve the Elven Ways. May the Universal Spirit burn deep within my spirit.*

Take the "pentacle" or "holed-stone" from the altar and go to the north. Trace your "Sign of Earth"* with the tool and see it green. As the portal opens, visualize a Sylvan Tree Elf emerge from the Otherworld (from the north) to join your ritual circle. It does not matter that you must at first envision or imagine these energetic events in your mind's eye. They are present even when we do not see them—just as much as there is electricity in the air and gravity accompanying condensed masses, we do not have to always "see" this unseen power to tap its potential. The energy is summoned in ritual by personally generating a like energy which is projected and will attract and exchange with other similar energies in kind. See the "Sign of Earth" blazing bright as you speak the Earth Key:

*Moh-ar Dee-ah-el Heh-keh-teh-gah. Ahd-hoo-ee Glee-im Awe-guhs Foil-chah nah*

---

\* A personal symbol, glyph or "*Sign of Portal*" aligned with the element. Examples appear in the forthcoming chapter on Self-Dedication.

*Speer-ohd-dee deh Cah-reeg en-duil-yah
Awe-guhs Tah-lave See-uh ar aye-it sho.
In the names of the Northern Quadrangle,
I call thee spirits and powers of stone, leaf,
land and the pentacle, to witness and de-
fend this rite, shield and protect this "Ma-
gick Sphere." King and Queen of the
Gnomes and Sylves, on this side of the
Sacred Circle are you invited.*

Go to the east and trace the "Sign of Air"
with the wand, envisioning it yellow or
purple. With the Air threshold veil lifted,
envision an emergence of a "Sylphen Fey"
coming to your circle from the (eastern)
Otherworld as you intone the Air Key:

*Oh-roh Ee-bah Ah-oh-zodpee. Ahd-hoo-ee
Glee-im Awe-guhs Foil-chah nah Speer-
ohd-dee deh Spay-er en-ghee-huh Awe-
guhs Nay-all See-uh ar aye-it sho. In the
names of the Eastern Quadrangle, I call
thee spirits and powers of the sky, wind,
air and wand. Shield and protect this
"Magick Sphere." King and Queen of the
Sylphs and Sprytes of the breeze and
flowers, on this side of the Sacred Circle
are you invited now.*

Bring with you to the south your "sword," 'sickle' or 'blade,' and trace your "Sigil of Fire" in the air with the tool, seeing it red. As you open the portal of the south, you see a draconian figure emerge from the Otherworld, coming forth to join your magickal rite as you speak the Fire Key:

*Oh-ee-peh Teh-ah-ah Peh-doh-keh. Ah-nahsh Glee-im Awe-gu-hs Foil-chah nah Speer-ohd-dee deh Gree-uhn Awe-guhs chin-nuh See-uh ar aye-it sho. In the names of the Southern Quadrangle, I call thee spirits and powers of the skystar, sun, flame and sword. Shield and protect this "Magick Sphere." King and Queen of the Fire-Drakes and Dragons, on this side of the Sacred Circle are you invited now.*

Take the 'cup' to the western direction and use it to trace the "Water Sign' and see it blue. From the west you can imagine merfolk, or 'undine,' appear from the Otherworld mists, as you intone the Water Key:

*Em-peh-heh Are-es-el Gah-ee-oh-leh. Ah-neer Glee-im Awe-gu-hs Foil-chah nah Speer-ohd-dee deh Gah-lahk En-oo-esh-ka Awe-guhs mwir-uh See-uh ar aye-it sho.*

*In the names of the Western Quadrangle, I call thee spirits and powers of the moon, sea, water and grail. Shield and protect this "Magick Sphere." King and Queen of the Merfolk of the wave, on this side of the Sacred Circle are you invited now.*

Leave each of your representations of the "Gifts of Faeire"—the "Elemental tools"—at their respective directions. After all these "keys" are activated, return to the altar (central workspace) and affirm:

*Guh Renv-en en-na Too-huh deh Dahn-non Bahn-ahk-tree or-een. Cos-eent en Nuh-dee-huh doh are aye-it show. Etz-are-peh. Heh-coh-mah. Nah-en-tah. Bee-toh-em. In the names of Akasha, Nyu, Spirit of the Quintessenal Fifth Element, I call the Spirits of the Tuatha D'Anu, the Danubian Sidhe, the Ancient and Shinning Ones. High Elves of the Otherworld, shield and protect this "Magick Sphere." Spirits of the Wood Elves, you too are invited to my Circle of Power.*

Visualize the boundary of the magic sphere clearly, as it descends into the ground beneath you and into the sky above. See its auric shield as a bright "force field" of light and energy complete with your "Sigils of Elemental Portals" burning brightly in each cardinal direction. Each of the Elementals called to the circle stand guard near their respective seals. Meditate on what is happening and hold the images clearly in your mind. Finally intone:

> *Elemental Spirits of the Otherworld shield and protect this "Magick Sphere." Be a witness now and co-magician in the magick I summon here in this Sacred Space. Guardians of the Universe, Watchers and Portal Messengers, come now to witness and aid in the celebration of Light and Love enacted here in my ceremony. May the grace and blessing of the Source of All Being and Creation pervade in my spirit forever and always.*

The "Circle of Power" or "*Nemeton*" is now ready for magickal work. Remember to "Extinguish the Powers of the Magick Sphere" before completing your ceremony and departing from your Sacred Space—as given in the next section.

# extinguishing the circle of power

In every tradition that casts or summons a "Circle of Power," there is a similar concluding rite where all energies called *in* during the ritual are thanked and dismissed. Elemental energies used for crafting or casting the "Circle of Power" must be extinguished too. This is an important formality maintained by Elvish Wizards and Druids. Without a ceremonial manner of etiquette for opening a circle so closed, there is nothing to distinguish the Sacred Space or *Nemeton* from the ordinary surrounding space. The "Magick Sphere" exists as a psychological and spiritual thought-formed boundary to confine and focus the energy channeled by the Wizard. It has a second purpose—as a "Circle of Protection" for Wizards when they are channeling raw energy currents. And finally, it represents a fractal reality, as discussed previously.

To open a circle sealed by magick—or otherwise extinguish the powers of the circle so cast—move around the boundary of the circle counter-clockwise, thanking and dismissing the Elementals while retrieving the tools left there. If you have traced any sigils, lore suggests that you retrace them in reverse—"erasing" them and closing the portals that they access—even if they are "only" mental doorways for a novice—you usually don't want to leave these "open."

If you began (or oriented) your *Nemeton* to the north (Earth Element), then you will want to finish there—so begin in the west. If you started in the east, begin extinguishing in the north—always working backwards, counter-clockwise ("*tuathal*") when opening the circle at the end of a rite. Use the following formal incantations in the order most appropriate to your needs.

WEST: *Slahn Ah-we-leh Speer-ohd-dee deh Gah-lahk En-oo-eesh-kah Awe-guhs Mwir-uh. Guh-rehv Mee-luh mah Ah-guhv. Depart in peace Western spirits of moon, sea, water and grail. May the energies of the Water Element return to your place of dwelling until you are again called.*

SOUTH: *Slahn Ah-we-leh Speer-ohd-dee deh Ghree-uhn Awe-guhs Chin-Nuh. Guh rehv Mee-luh mah Ah-guhv. Depart in peace Southern spirits of skystar, flame, sun and blade. May the energies of the Fire Element return to your place of dwelling until you are again called.*

EAST: *Slahn Ah-we-leh Speer-ohd-dee deh Spay-ir En-ghee-huh Awe-guhs Nay-ahl. Guh rehv Mee-luh mah Ah- guhv. Depart in peace Eastern spirits of sky, wind, air and wand. May the energies of the Air Element return to your place of dwelling until you are again called.*

NORTH: *Slahn Ah-we-leh Speer-ohd-dee deh Cah-reeg En-duil-yuh Awe-guhs Taw-luhv. Guh rehv Mee-luh mah Ah-guhv. Depart in peace Northern spirits of leaf, land, stone and pentacle. May the energies of the Earth Element return to your place of dwelling until you are again called.*

When the final ritual tools are retrieved, bring them back to your central working space and address the Universe with:

*Slahn Ah-we-luh En-too-huh deh Dahn-non Awe-guhs. Guh rehv Mee-luh mah Ah-guhv. Skee-uh deh Dree-uckt Show. Many thanks and blessings to the spirits who have gathered here. Depart in peace spirits of the Tuatha D'Anu, Wood Elves, Sidhe, and all Ancient and Shinning Ones who have blessed me with your mystical presence. Return to the Sidhe Hills and Faerie Dwellings until you are again called forth. May the grace of the rays of the Source of All Being and Creation go with all who have come to join in this magickal work. I depart in peace to my place of dwelling until I return here again in magick's hour. The Magick Sphere stands open now, but is never broken. Awen (Ah-oo-een).*

With these last words, the energies of the circle itself are extinguished. You may raise your arms and see the bluish-white energy of the "magick sphere" burn brightly—and then as you quickly lower your arms, see these energies of the *Nemeton* ground and fade.

# consecrating the symbols of power or "gifts of faeire"

This rite may be used for "charging" or "consecrating" ritual tools—particularly "Elemental tools" representing the *Gifts of Faeire*." It may also be used to ceremonially charge amulets and talismans for other magical purposes. Essentially, all implements or "tools" of magic must be consecrated— dedicated and "charged" for "magickal" purposes—prior to incorporation into ritual and ceremony. Otherwise they are simply mundane objects. A "Magickal tool" is so considered because a Wizard is able to use it to connect to the energy that the tool represents—or is a catalyst for. Remember: *like forces attract like forces* in magic.

**CONSECRATING THE SYMBOLS OF POWER**

Conjure your "Circle of Power"—then say:

*May peace and love fill my spirit so I may be a beacon of light and life projecting such energy outward in all directions of the Universe. May the Ancient and Shinning Ones hear my call. I ask the spirits of the Earth who are friendly to the Elven Ways to join me in consecrating this sacred icon to thy tradition. Come now and bless this [name(s) of talisman(s) to be consecrated], so that you will more easily recognize it when I present it to you in the future.*

You will need your item(s) available when you conduct the ritual. This simplified rite should be used only for "Elemental tools" or if not, an item that is used for more than a single-use "spell." For example, you might charge a runic pendant to attract love energy into your life, but Elven Wizardry is not used to gain the specific love of so-and-so, such as you might find in a targeted love-spell. True "Elvish Magick" is timeless and not restricted to a specific event or person (usually) and therefore the construction of general talismans that attract love would are more appropriate for this rite than a "love spell." Other examples may just as easily be applied here.

When the tool is "ready"—assuming it was

just constructed—say:

> *Hail to the Sidhe, the High Ones, and to the Sylvanus, the Sylphs and Sylves and the Wood Elves themselves. Hail to the Lords and Ladies of the Land, Sky, and Sea. Greetings to all Creatures of Faerie—all ye welcomed here. Mark well what you witnessed this day/eve and remember. May the Eternal Source of Everpresent Light, look favorably on the magick I conceive.*

In order for this consecration to be effective, you must charge the item with your intentions. This requires some proficiency in the ability of energy channeling. For those eyes falling upon this with no prior experience, you are bidden by these words read here now—to never misuse what is discovered in our grimoires of rites and secret spells. By *this oath* between us I will offer the clue needed to make this work...

In this practice of magic, you need to feel (and "see") your thought-form, goal or Elemental current clearly outside of yourself. Breathe this energy—or aetheric matter—in and feel it completely wash through your body as you absorb it through your every pore. Feel it run through your entire circulatory system. You are Assimilating this energy in total—so it had better be 'positive' or for your 'highest good'—and focus it on your arms and hands; project it from within and release (or push) it into the 'item'.

Take your "symbol of power" to the north with the "bowl of salt." Set the bowl on the "pentacle"—or Earth-stone (unless you are consecrating your Earth-tool for the first time, then the ground will work) and set the item in the bowl of salt and/or sprinkling some of the salt on it saying:

> *Look here and witness ye Spirits of the North. By sprinkling this [n.] with the Salt of the Earth do I consecrate it by the names and Seals of the Earth Element.*

Take your "symbol of power" to the southeast, bringing your "incense burner" with, and if there is not already sufficient smoke, add more incense resin. For this rite you will want to select an essence to burn that correlates with the talisman or purpose of the rite. Pass it through the smoke and say:

> *Look here and witness ye Spirits of the East and South. I pass this [n.] through burning herbal resins that waft through the air. In doing so I now consecrate it by the ancient names and seals of the elements Air and Fire.*

Continue your clockwise movement to the western direction, and use your "bowl of water"—or *'sacred vessel'*—to sprinkle some of the water onto the "symbol of power" saying:

> *Look here and witness ye Spirits of the West. I pass this [n.] through your realm by sprinkling it with your water of life and renewal. By the secret names of the Sea do I consecrate this symbol as witnessed by the Water Element.*

If consecrating symbols representing "Gifts of Faeire" using this rite, it is customary to call on—and charge the tool—with energies appropriate to the original *Tuatha d'Anu* artifacts. ["Faeire" is an archaic spelling, applied here just as in the original handwritten manuscript.]

## "THE GIFTS OF FAEIRE"

- Stone of Fal—North/Earth, Master Morfessas
- Spear of Lugh—East/Air, Master Esras
- Sword of Nuada—South/Fire, Master Uscias
- Cauldron of Dagda—West/Water, Master Semias

An 'item' is ritually consecrated prior to its use (or ritual application) as a sacred tool— but, there is no strict arcane dogma concerning how long tools will hold a charge— or how a blatant recharge is necessary, if at all. Items will also take on a charge 'naturally' over time with regular use as focal instruments. Gems and metal objects tend to hold a charge longest; followed by wood; then liquid.

# the basic rites of faerie-calling

The "Children of Faerie" do not submit themselves to the will of Wizards like those spirits conjured and encountered from medieval grimoires—which are in actuality thought-formed ancestral and cosmic extensions of ourselves and our own consciousness as One with the ALL. "Children of Faerie" will certainly not so easily cater to Human whims. Thus, there is no ritual or ceremony that will ensure "conjuration" of the "Elven-Ffayrie" beings.

However, various methods are hidden in esoteric lore of Druidism and surviving remnants of those teachings of the Elven Wizards and Mystics once restricted to initiates of the "Ancient Mystery School." Therefore, what we may include here are "suggestions" to entice, gain favor or otherwise develop working relationships with nature-bound spirits. This is a prerequisite for any ceremonial or "at will" contact in Elven Wizard traditions. Of course, magical work of this nature will require access to the physical "Green World"—where you believe "nature spirits" reside. You need not even bother with this in a purely urban setting where you are almost guaranteed to find disappointment.

Once initial contact is made, initiating it in the future is increasingly easier—and more innate—with each success. When a relationship has commenced, be sure to ask the spirit(s) their names (and signs) and their preferred method of future contact. This is the only manner by which Fey-Touched Humans become privy to a true mystical apprenticeship with the Elven-Ffayrie far surpassing what has been considered "acceptable" by *them* for me to print in this tome.

I am permitted only inclusion lore that will be used by *them* to test *you* as a potential initiate. We should expect that they will certainly screen potential "Elf-Friends" and "Ffayrie-Allies." So as to safeguard our own existent Oaths, the *Elvenomicon* series is prepared as an objective mystical guide—relaying to potential initiates Nature's own "recruiting manual" for an awakening available to those truly enlightened folk that have not fully invalidated and forgotten who they are in a world of depersonalization and disenchantment.

If you are reading these words in the dark half of the year, you may still have time to prepare an initial rite of contact on a forthcoming Beltane or Midsummer. For this you will need a "Silver Wand"—an apple-wood wand with three silver bells hanging from white ribbon. It should be consecrated prior to this rite. Use this wand to conjure your circle. Then, starting in the northeast, sprinkle "Primrose flower petals"—moving *deosil* around the boundary of your circle, As you say:

> *Under stone, under sea, under every blade of grass. In the winds, in the flames, in the circle that I cast. Elf and Ffayrie, come to me. Grant me favor and be blest.*

Ignite your incense coals in your sand-filled "cauldron" or "burner" at the south-west. Heap on some incense—an herb-and-twig mixture followed by sweet-smelling resins —and feel the smoke radiating from your "Magick Sphere" and into the Otherworld dimension, acting as a beacon to your call:

> *I have studied the way of Sidhe. I shall awaken every tree. I have called to share my home, with Undina, Sylpha, Elf and Gnome. I emerge from a world of mortal strife, here to partake in Faerie life.*

Prepare three small "shot glasses" in the northwest with "elderberry wine" or "milk and honey." Set out 'sweetbreads' or "cookies" alongside this. Then, take up your "bowl of salt"; sprinkle a circular boundary around the food offering as you speak:

> *Gifts of Faeire granted me, Elemental tools here on display. Now a gift I give to thee, to ignite a bond 'tween you and me. Overnight I'll leave this food, in hopes we'll meet here some day.*

Remains of the food may be removed the next day. Essences of the offering will already have been taken—or not. The physical food itself may or may not. "Nature spirits" also send their animal allies to feast on the physical foodstuff once they have accepted the sentiment of the gift. Typically, Elvish Wizards will make regular food offerings to the Otherworld Fey—and a particular location at regular intervals. "Circles of Power" for the sole intention of calling the Elven-Ffayrie spirits may be consecrated or conjured differently. Elemental callings may even be modified to meet the needs of contacting members of the Sylvanus Folk—those maintain their own Elemental hierarchy. The following are the suggestions listed in the original Elven-Faerie Grimoire:

## SYLVANUS CORRESPONDENCES

EAST : Air Element—"Tree Elves"

SOUTH : Fire Element—"Sprytes"

WEST : Water Element—"Mushroom Fey"

NORTH : Earth Element—"Woodland Gnomes"

ELF-KING : "Lord Oberon" (Auberon)

FAERIE-QUEEN : "Lady Titania"

In your woodland travels or spiritual walks in the forests, valleys and mountain ranges throughout the Middle World, you may very well find something in Nature that your inner voice tells you is a gateway threshold to the Otherworld. At these places you can conjure a circle for the purposes of Faerie-calling but be advised: do not disturb the physical environment; do not make a lot of noise; and keep ritual incantations to a minimal and lighthearted—which is why many of those included in this book seem so whimsical. Keep them directed specifically toward "nature spirits." You might speak something like:—

*I am a spirit of peace. Let peace ring throughout the entire Universe. May my energy and vibration be that only of peace, love and harmony that I extend to the Creatures of Elphame. Know that I [your magickal name] come to you in admiration and respect. I seek contact and initiation to your Otherworld, in grace and goodness. I shall not disturb, trespass or break the solemn vows shared between us. I seek to be your companion and will adhere to the boundaries of that friendship. By the grace of the All-Source, please come forth and make thyself known.*

Elven-Ffayrie lore suggests that animals as messengers of the Otherworld. Some are considered "more sacred" or more iconic to specific aspects of the tradition than others —but *all* woodland, marine and flying creatures are sacred as representing interconnection of All life as "One" in the Universe with ALL life—meaning that all life is one and equal at the Source of All Being.

Animals maintain a role, almost as if ambassadors, negotiators or again, "messengers" between the "World of Men" and the "World of Nature"—or the physical visible world and the unseen Otherworld. As a general species the Humans have not treated their stewardship of Earth with due respect —nor is it it shown to our animal brethren as it should be. Working with animals in both the physical world and in the spirit realm (or astral) may even grant favorable attitudes toward you from the fey.

# an introduction to elven-faerie spells

Elven Wizards and Druids create their own unique 'prayers', which others might just as easily call "spells"—and still there are others that refer to it as "creative visualization therapy." Our minds, the *Self* and its interconnection to the All, may be described in various ways, names and traditions. We are most concerned with techniques that do yield results—regardless of various methodologies and semantics applied to the same use of "Cosmic Law" for thousands of years.

"Elven-Faerie Spells" may be created by an individual for any particular need or occasion. Remember: "magick" to Elves is a creative art—one that the Masters take great pride in. In order to "write your own magick," however, you should be acquainted and proficient with traditional rites and the rules of spellcraft.

Additional information is also available in companion volumes of this series: *"Elven-Faerie Spellbook"* and *"The Enchanted Forest."*

A "spell" is a small act or short magickal working performed in a "Circle of Power" in order to bring about a desired result or movement of energy toward a certain direction. This does not necessarily occur immediately; it may take days, weeks, months and even years (in some instances) to manifest—depending on the situation.

Most common uses of "Faerie Spellcraft" include protection, fertility and abundance, prosperity and wealth, and the banishment of negativity and/or warding away of unwanted energy. There are many other uses of magick—such as the ever popular "single use love spell," which is not dealt with in this tradition of magick. According to lore, the most popular days for magical work in the Elven tradition are "Elf Day"or "Tree Day" (*Tuesday*) and "Fey Day" (*Saturday*).

Every day is *magical*. Each of the planet-oriented days of the week represent attributes connected to a "ray" of the "Elven Star"— which allows us to glean the Sevenfold Schema of the original source tradition in the *Ancient Near East*. Note here: there are seven days—thus seven colors, seven notes of music and naturally seven (6+1) points on the "Elven Star" are all correlated within the paradigm of Elven Tradition.

---

SEVENFOLD SCHEMA (or ELVEN STAR)

Monday: Moonday; blue; "G" note; pearl stone; silver.

Tuesday: Elf Day/Tree Day; red; "C"; ruby; iron.

Wednesday: Woden's Day; orange; "D"; opal; mercury.

Thursday: Thor's Day; indigo; "A"; sapphire; tin.

Friday: Freya's Day; green; "F"; emerald; copper.

Saturday: Fey Day; violet; "B"; onyx; lead.

Sunday: Sun Day; yellow; "E"; diamond; gold.

---

Herbs sometimes appear in lore as "Elf Amulets." Acorns aid in fertility rites—and those found by moonlight are symbols of prosperity and abundance. Acorns are essentially the fruit and seed of the oak tree and carry a history of traditional use for fertility, love, and protective spells and charms. They should, unless otherwise advised, always be gathered in daylight hours, preferably at noon. Keep your chosen intention for the amulet in the mind while collecting them.

In ceremonial magick, wands made from oak are often capped with a large acorn tip. Cones (pine, &tc.) may also be used for this —making excellent tools of growth magic.

In divination for "love," a couple may each drop an acorn in still water and watch to see how they respond to each other.

In a spell to encourage a friend to initiate a romantic interest, seven acorns are placed on a small square of white cloth and tied up with a red cord or ribbon to form an "amulet bag." After sleeping with it under their pillow for three consecutive nights, it is buried beneath a rose bush and then the person calls out for the other to come. The acorn is also a nut-food or it may be crushed into "oak flour."

Apple-seeds are natural items of love-drawing magic—though also poisonous in large quantities. The common apple tree is actually a hybrid effort—the result of years of crossbreeding to bring us the familiar fruit we know today. The original apple species—the crab apple (*malus hupehensis*)—produces much smaller fruits, resembling cherries. The *Rosaceae* family of apples is shared by over 3,000 different species, including the ash, bay/laurel, cherry, hawthorn, peach and plum trees. In Druid folklore, apple is also associated with *Queris* or *Quert Ogham* and is the traditional wood of love magick.

Most Celtic scholars associate apples with the Isle of Avalon, called *"Emain Ablach,"* which some also interpret as "Isle of Glass." In fact *"Affalon"* may be a mutation of "Appleland"—perhaps an ancient orchard or grove. One famous magical tool in lore—referred to previously—the Celtic shaman's wand, called the *"craebh ciuil"* or "Silver Branch," was fashioned from apple-wood. The fruit is also sacred to Mystics because it bares the image of a pentagram when cut at its midsection, and is particularly significant to the harvest—the festivals of Lughnassadh and the autumn equinox. In ancient times, the harvest traditionally began with a toast of cider. At Yule, apple-wine *"wassail"* is used ceremonially for tree blessing. Apples are found in natural healing remedies for anemia and are good sources of Vitamins A and E, which may assist purifying from toxins and lowering blood pressure.

According to faerie lore, bay leaves ward away the enchantments, spells and glamour of others when placed under the tongue. Pine-cones—when found by moonlight—are symbols of good fortune, health and well-being. Perhaps the most famous herbal 'Elf-Amulet' is the *"trefoil,"* *"trifolium,"* *"shamrock"* or "clover" that is so commonly identified as a symbol of luck—or to ward away warfare. All herbs require cutting or removal from the land, so it is customary to "ask the plant's permission" in order to officiate an understanding that a spiritual intelligence exists within all life. A common incantation of the "magical herbalist" is:

*"With this strike may you grow stronger."*

"Magical herbalists" have also designated specific herbs that are held particularly sacred in Elven-Ffayrie Magickal Tradition. These include: dandelion root; chamomile; mistletoe; elder flow'r: hops; Irish moss; rosemary; rose-hips; raspberry leaf; mint; mullien; skullcap; and slippery elm bark. These may be used by themselves or in conjunction with each other for attracting the attention of "Otherworldly folk" in ritual as well as mixed with black tea and drank as an infusion. They calming herbs—and they may aid one in attuning to the energies of the "Green World" and "Faerielands."

To protect a home, an Elvish shaman might use sage and fern to clear out negative energy. Personal sigils of protection could be traced on the four outer walls to conjure a "magick shield." One might use the "Elf-Sign" (star) or a protective 'rune', 'Ogham' —even the "Dragon's Eye"—will generally suffice for banishing and warding against "typical" types of unfriendly (or malignant) energy. A traditional Gaelic-Welsh incantation for this purpose is:

> *Cosaint agus beanachtai yn n'Deith do talamh seo. Dibir na ole agus dona.*

Ask the aid of "helpful" Elementals. Decide and fix on a target or energy current (or ray) that you wish to block. Envision a representation of the unwanted energy or current and feel that it is the embodiment of what are you are warding away. See the auric energy projected from it/them as being blocked or shielded—as if encased in a bubble—which dissolves into nothingness as you say:

*I command you, by the names and letters of the Most High, to depart in peace!*

Keys to effective spellcraft are: clarity of intention; the ability to raise internal energy and merge it with assisting external ones; visualization of desired goals clearly; and the willpower to properly release energy so summoned from within and without. The keys—in this order—form the fundamental steps taken in all practices of "spellcraft." The following are some additional tips to aid your faerie spell-weaving:

—Incorporate only tools and items of a "like energy" to that which you wish to connect with. All others are distractions.

—Visualization skills make-or-break your mystical prowess of directing energy with the Mind, according to Cosmic Law.

—Only call forth or summon spirits and energies specific to your purpose; and only those that accelerate your cause.

—Ask the "Universe" (and/or "spirit guides") to assist carrying ("channeling") or directing release of energies via the appropriate channels.

—Do not dwell on a ritual working already performed, or on what the nature of the results will be, for at least three days afterward. This keeps any energy used for that ritual-spell "out there" "working for you" and not contained or restricted to the vicinity of your thoughts locally.

—Most importantly, it is essential that you believe in your abilities. Remember the ancient proverb that: *all intentional Self-determined acts are magical.*

# the elven wizardry of healing and protection

Consecrate a "Circle of Power" in a place receiving blessing, protection and/or healing. Set out your ceremonial tools—or representations of the "Gifts of Faeire"—in their correlating directions. Enter the circle from the northeast by procession if there are multiple practitioners. Go to the center of your workspace unless you are working in a group that allows for using "Elemental Stations." Light a white candle and say:

*"May there be peace within my being."*

Each participant should do the same. You can then proceed to address each of the directions from the center (altar)—or if performed in a group, other participants may be stationed at each Elemental "quarter."

NORTH: *May peace ring out and extend across northern expansions.*

EAST: *May peace ring out in the east and extend across the furthest plains.*

SOUTH: *May peace ring out in the south and extend to the peaks of the tallest mountains.*

WEST: *May peace ring out in the west and extend to the depths of the deepest sea.*

Light more white candles—as well as a blue and a red one if this rite is for "healing." You may even state affirmations as you light them, before continuing with the rite.

NORTH: *May peace, love and harmony extend to every living being and space in the Universe, especially [name of what/ who is to be blessed/protected/healed]. Great Bear of the North, I call now on your strength and the wisdom of the Earth Element. Offer your blessing towards me and extend your protective/healing power on [n].*

EAST: *May the purity of the Air Element enrich all work performed here. May the Winds aid me in purifying the energies of [n]. Hawk of the Eastern Dawn, I call now on your agility and the wisdom of the Sky Element. Offer your blessing toward me and extend your protective/healing power towards [n].*

*SOUTH: May the purifying flame purge and annihilate that which is unclean, especially in this place/for [n]. Great Stag of Southern Flame, I call on your virility and the wisdom of the Fire Element. Offer your blessing toward me and extend your protective/healing power towards [n].*

*WEST: May the blessing of the purifying and healing powers of the transforming waters be upon me in the work that I do towards [n]. Wise Salmon of the Western Sea, I call upon thy True Knowledge and the wisdom of the Water Element. Offer your blessing toward me and extend your protective/ healing power towards [n].*

Return to the center of your workspace and recite the "Elvish Wizard's Benediction"— or the "Gorsedd Prayer" of Druidism. You may use a version from some other ceremonial source or the more commonly known one, provided here:

*Dyro, Dduw, dy naw erth, deall Ae yn heal gybod; Ae yng n gwybod, gwybod y cyfi-*

*awn; Ae yng ngwybod y cyfiawn; Eigarn Ac a garu, caru pobhanfod; Ac ym mhob hanfod caru Duw. Duw a phob dai oni.*

*Grant us O God, thy protection; and in protection, strength; and in strength understanding; and in understanding, perception; and in perception, the perception of righteousness; and in the perception of righteousness, the love of it; and in the love of it, the love of all life; and in the love of all life, the love of God and all goodness.*

*May the Source of All Being and Creation extend currents/rays to protect/heal this place/person.*

Bless the "target" with "saltwater" and "burning incense." A "smudge-stick" of sage, reed or fern might also be used. Bless the "bowl of water" and sprinkle it on the person and around the person, or in each room of the house and around the outside of the property. With the "salt-water," say at each point:

*By the Elemental Powers of Earth and Water do I so cleanse and consecrate [n].*

With the incense, at each point:

*By the Elemental Powers of Flame and Wind do I so purify and bless [n].*

Returning to the center of the circle, complete this portion of the rite by saying:

*May there be peace [in this home/at this place/with this person]. May it/they absorb the protection/healing channeled to this space "now made sacred" [or if at the Grove, "most sacred"].*

If there is a faerie-shaman or Druid present, they may wish to seek the nature of an ailment of a person—or the energetic disturbance of an area—by communicating with Otherworld "shadows," "spirit guides" or other kind of energy work that allows for astral communication. Supplemental healing and protection spells may be performed here. Once the ceremonial goals are satisfied, thank the powers and extinguish the energies of the "Magick Sphere."

# self-dedication rite

Regardless of whether or not you formally decide to join (or develop) a "coven," "circle" or "grove" of the Elven Tradition — whatever name you use to call such a close-knit magical group—you will first need to perform a personal "Self-Dedication" rite to the Elven Way.

Dedication rites are traditionally different from "initiations," because a dedication rite is performed in solitary—while alone in the woods or wilderness. This ceremony is not necessarily a "magickal spell" in the traditional sense—it is a personal "Rite of Passage" observed much like the "seasonal celebrations" of the "Wheel of the Year."

The Self-Dedication Ceremony is a form of psychological magic—it effectively changes an internal set or mode of thinking that determines our perspective in life. One such premise for a true Self-Dedication Ceremony: the Elven Wizard—or Elvish Wizard-*to-be*—has just discovered some strange arcane tome, such as the one you currently hold, and realizes —or awakens to a realization—that either they personally share the Elven-Faerie-Dragon legacy themselves, or for some "unknown" reason, they feel a peculiar inclination to these mysteries, innately drawn to the path via self-initiation.

Although this rite did not appear at the beginning of the original "Elven-Faerie Grimoire"—which the current author has made every effort to relay here in proper tribute —it would be logical that this is among the first, if not *the first*, ceremonial observation made by a practicing Seeker (since it may be performed without 'tools').

Focused concentration, meditation and self-dedication rites performed in Nature may aid in bridging a relationship with the natural, spiritual, or otherwise "metaphysical" side of Reality. All skill and ability is accumulated over time as a result of consistent growth of this relationship, which breaks down the artificial barriers of fragmented separation between the *Self* and the *Cosmos* —what is considered "Magical Authority" or "Power," but which is really derived from the ability to operate the *Self* in perfect clarity—or what we call "*Self-Honesty*."

Conjure the "Magick Sphere"—or *Nemeton*—in a manner that you have practiced—even if you have only envisioned doing so in your mind, as you read this "grimoire," which is a form of magic in itself when energy is properly directed. This time, as you move about to trace the boundary of the circle, by hand (or wand), you will set out an "Elemental Candle" at each cardinal direction—a common practice in all forms of Elemental Magick and Wizardry. Choose one of an appropriate Elemental color for each direction. Wait until you address each Element during the Self-Dedication Rite to light the candles. Use incantations from the "Casting the Circle of Power" section of this grimoire only after performing a "self-dedication."

Once the area is deemed "Sacred Space," go to the center of the circle—you do not need an "altar" for this rite—and stand or kneel, facing north, saying:

*In my mortal form I am known as* [given name] *but today/tonight I come to you in my Elven-Ffayrie form with the name* [a chosen magical name]. *I come to you now, Spirits of the Universe as an "Elf-*

*Child*" ["*Fae-Child*" (female); and "*Elf-Friend*" for mortal practitioners who are not certain they personally represent the Elven-Faerie legacy.]

Take a "bowl of salt" and remove a pinch, placing it on your tongue. Feel the salt of the Earth entering your bloodstream and becoming a part of your entire body as you say:

*I am a child of Earth. I am a child of the stars. I have studied on my own in preparation, but now I seek the Spirits of Nature to be my teacher, to instructor me in the true sciences of the Cosmos. Hidden in your folds lies the answers of Creation and Life. We are one. I am one with the entire Universe. I seek to share a relationship with thee.*

Stand and move to the north, light a "green candle," saying:

*Spirits of the Enchanted Forest, of plants and rocks and trees, awaken and know me* [magical name]. *I come with peace within, seeking your aid in learning thy mysteries. I vow to ever uphold thy secrets,*

> *walking the path of wisdom and enlightenment. I present myself to this magic circle as a follower of the Elven Ways.*

Trace a seal or symbol of the Earth Element that you will use regularly in your rites to incite energetic activity of the Elements.

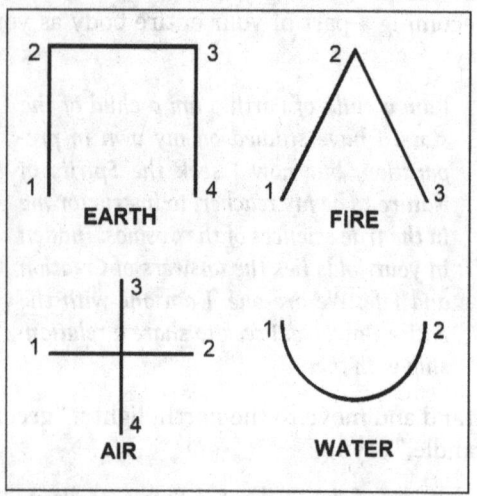

Examples shown here are based on the traditional Druidic interpretation of Elemental Magick. Envision the "Sign of Earth" as green in color, as you intone:

*By this Sign shall we know each other.*

Go to the east; while lighting the "yellow candle," say:

*Spirits of the Enchanted Breeze, of winds and sky and Air, awaken and know me [magical name]. I come with peace within, seeking your aid in learning thy mysteries. I vow to ever uphold thy secrets, walking the path of wisdom and enlightenment. I present myself to this magic circle as a follower of the Elven Ways.*

Trace your "Sigil of Air," envisioning it yellow, saying:

*By this Sign shall we know each other.*

Move to the south and speak the following as you light the "red candle" there:

*Spirits of the Enchanted Mountain, of sun and star and flame, awaken and know me [magical name]. I come with peace within, seeking your aid in learning thy mysteries. I vow to ever uphold thy secrets, walking the path of wisdom and enlightenment. I present myself to this magic circle as a follower of the Elven Ways.*

Trace your "Fire Sign" and see it red, saying:

> *By this Sign shall we know each other.*

Move to address the west, light the "blue candle" and say:

> *Spirits of the Enchanted Sea, of waves and lakes and rain, awaken and know me [magickal name]. I come with peace within, seeking your aid in learning thy mysteries. I vow to ever uphold thy secrets, walking the path of wisdom and enlightenment. I am a follower of the Elven Ways.*

Trace your "Seal of Water" in blue as you intone:

> *By this Sign shall we know each other.*

Return to the center and take some anointing oil—a type of your personal choosing. Spiritual traditions teach to "anoint" with oil from the feet to the head (upward)—and bless (wash) from head to foot (downward). Anoint your feet and say:

> *Blessed be the feet that bring me here this*

*day/night and enable me to touch the ground, to walk the path of the Ancients, treading the 'Right Way' always, never deviating from the path of enlightenment and wisdom.*

Anoint your knees, saying:

*Blessed be the knees that bend to give reverence to the Higher Power of the Universe, to the Source of All Being in the Cosmos that gives me the strength to move forth on the path of light and the ability to make or break my stride.*

Anoint the palms of your hands and say:

*Blessed be the hands that lift in praise of the Universe and all Life. They are my commanding hands I raise in power and I acknowledge their ability to direct my will, as they are extensions of my active mind.*

Anoint the heart—left breast—saying:

*Blessed be the flame that burns within my heart, that I may know the True Love of the Universe and in so doing, that I may recognize the Right Way by what I feel deeply burning in my very spirit.*

Anoint the lips and say:

*Blessed be the lips that speak the sacred words of incantation. May the words they speak only advance my evolution further and never idle or in vain. From my mouth, I utter the words of power and share in the breath of the All, yet remaining silent to non-believers.*

Finally, speak the following as you anoint your forehead:

*Blessed be the mind that seeks to understand its own nature and connection to the true Self, that allows me the ability to seek true knowledge and guidance from my true Self into this body, which is at one with my mind. Let my thoughts be pure and only of a nature that will contribute positively to my Ascension.*

Elven Wizards and Mystics often consecrate a personal item, emblem or artifact—like a pendant or necklace—which is later worn as a symbol of dedication to the Elven Way. Hold up your talisman saying:

*May the Spirits of Nature and the Universe beyond, see and bless this symbol of my dedication—recognizing it and me in our future exchanges.*

Thank the energies called to the rite and extinguish the circle, completing the ceremony.

# circle-initiation rite

"Sylvan Magick" is mainly related to trees and so groups of practitioners coming together to learn and practice the Elven Way will often call themselves a "grove" instead of a "coven." Magick may certainly be performed solitary, but 'circle magic' or 'group magick' generally requires a minimum of three people—one to represent each of the most basic Elemental Stations: Land, Sky and Sea. Traditional 'Elemental schema' run as high as nine different "*duile*" or Elemental aspects that participants may occupy as 'Stations' without dividing the system further. Larger groups may designate tree or "Ogham" names for a larger 'outer circle' of practitioners if necessary.

A "coven" or "grove" logically begins with members initiating each other. But this doesn't always make much sense at the initial inception of a group. In the past, the leader of a coven was so by her status; a leader of a grove or Arch Druid might be elected by a council. These High Priests and Priestesses are not "initiated" into their positions; they are "installed" into the group by other initiated members.

It is difficult in modern times to actually find a group using an authentic Elven-Faerie Tradition that is not diluted by the general pop-culture interpretations of Western Magickal Tradition. This is not surprising due to lack of true mainstream Elven-Faerie lore to draw such practices, especially those not restricted to a specific lineage or family tradition. With a rising underground popularity of the *Elvenomicon* series, this may change in the future.

This following rite was adopted in 1998 by the *"Elven Fellowship Circle of Magick."* The area of initiation should be an outdoor *Nemeton*. Choose a place where the group can meet repeatedly and form a connection with this terrain over time. This place must allow for an absence of worldly distraction and the ability to practice rituals without the unnerving discovery from disruptive onlookers. Construct a *Nemeton* of stones, being sure the diameter is large enough for all participants. A group of three can often use a circle nine feet in diameter. Do not overlook the significance of the "Megalithic Yard" when constructing these henges. A single unit (1-MY) is equivalent to 2.72 feet, making appropriate ceremonial sites approximately 8.16 or 10.88 feet in diameter by this rule. Be creative.

A "Magician/Sponsor" leads a blindfolded "Initiate" to the northeast corner of the *Nemeton*, where the Leader—a group founder or other "ceremonial magician" hereafter referred to as the "Guardian of the Grove"—greets them. The "Guardian" stands in wait at the northeast threshold, holding a sword.

GUARDIAN OF THE GROVE: *Who is it there that you bring here to the very Gates of this sphere most sacred and secret?*

MAGICIAN/SPONSOR: *A child of Earth and Star seeking entrance—to be set on the path of our mysteries.*

GUARDIAN: *Do you then present this person to the Grove, vouching before us for their conduct and their dedication to our circle and the Elven Ways?*

SPONSOR: *I do. I sponsor this child of Earth and Star, and must take responsibility for them now . They remain in a state of darkness—blinded to the mysteries of our Nemeton.*

GUARDIAN: *Then, as Guardian of this Gateway, I open the Portal to our Sphere —but it is never broken. You may enter this time by the Unspeakable Password.*

The "Magician/Sponsor" guides the "Initiate" to the center of the circle, where they are set before the existing membership of the Grove.

GUARDIAN: *Answer, Initiate. Do you seek entrance into the mysteries of the "Elven Fellowship Circle of Magick"* [or another name for your personal group]?

INITIATE: *I do.*

GUARDIAN: *Answer, Initiate. Do you come here of your own free will, free from the pressures of peers or others and free of ulterior motives?*

INITIATE: *I do.*

GUARDIAN: *And finally, answer, again: Are you willing to swear an oath to the secrecy by the ancient covenant of the Mystic Wizards of the Earth now raised before you, and this Council, and the spirits we have called to our nemeton?*

INITIATE: *I do.*

GUARDIAN: *Kneel and submit yourself to this Elven Druid Council.*

The "Initiate" kneels and the "Guardian of the Grove" begins to encircle them in *deosil* rotation—drawing up the primal energies of the Earth planet.

GUARDIAN: *You are now entering deep woods, the Enchanted World of the Elven-Faerie unsolicited. You step foot on the ground held most sacred to the Keepers of the Earth that maintain and celebrate the ancient Ways. Under penalty of death, no mortal shall step foot on our court unbidden, and thus you now render yourself to the mercy of the Court. You enter a place that is not a place in a time apart from time and still you are here. Fear has no place in our world—here in the Other-*

*world—and it is our will that you should perish from the spear-blades and arrowheads aimed at you by our Elven military as a sentence for such blasphemy. If you bring mortal fear in your heart to our world, you will undoubtedly summon your demise. How do you enter our world, Initiate?*

INITIATE: *With perfect love and perfect trust.*

GUARDIAN: *I ask the Sponsor: has this Initiate been properly prepared? Has s/he completed their Self-Dedication to the Elven Way? Is the Initiate recognized by the Elemental Portal Guardians of the Watchtowers?*

SPONSOR: *They are prepared. They are dedicated. They are recognized by the Elemental Realms.*

GUARDIAN: *We shall find out. May the Source of All Being and Creation grant us protection; and in protection, strength; and in strength, peace; and in peace, understanding; and in understanding, knowledge; and in knowledge, wisdom; and in wisdom, love; and in love, the love of all things; and in the love of all things, the love of the Universe.*

The "Sponsor" summons the "Initiate" up from their knees, guiding them on a cross-quarter Elemental journey before returning the center again. In ancient times, this would have been conducted in a cave or underground labyrinth. This text is read as the "Sponsor" guides them first to the south, as the "Guardian" reads from the center of the circle:

*In the beginning was the infinite void of Nothing, a canvas with no form, a screen without picture. But then came Light, the Dragon, the Cosmic Law, that which gave all existence its form, waves of potentiality sprawling across the matrix-fabric of the Universe.*

The "Initiate" is brought to the east:

*When the fires of life burned down to glowing embers, they breathed into existence the Air, the element of knowledge, and the Elven-Ffayrie spirits of the trees and breeze.*

Across to the west:

> *More and more tangible did the formless Spirit of Light become, when the Waters emerged, ripples sent out to every corner of all encompassing sea. But the currents of energy chased one another and became even more solid.*

And, around to the north:

> *The Formless Fire gave birth to Air; the gaseous Air gave way to water. The sea would yield finally to the land, to the Element of Earth, a powerfully strong and stable foundation to hold up the less tangible manifestations. This Earth is the planetary spirit of G'ea and She has had 'Keepers' and 'Guardians' at all times and places to maintain the balance of the Elemental World and thwart all that would cause disharmony on Earth.*

Returning to the center:

> *As you have come to us in the darkness of ignorance, know that we are the 'Keepers of the Earth,' the 'Guardians of the Green World' and 'Scions of the Secret Know-*

ledge' *from the ancients. As you emerge, reborn into a realm of Light and enchantment, your existing name is no longer appropriate and is retired at the boundary of the Sacred Grove. We shall know you as* [circle name for the Initiate]. *Welcome Elf/Ffayrie Child, Lord/Lady* [n].

The blindfold is removed. Existing members come forth and greet the Initiate, followed by a celebration in their honor.

# eisteddfodd liturgy

The *Nemeton* may be conjured by means already suggested, an astral version thereof, a mixture of "Casting" and "Group Liturgies," or simply by using this rite alone. Some incantations used in solitary Ritual Magic are not necessary to observe seasonal *Alardana* celebrations or "rites of passage." The liturgy presented here is named for a gathering of Welsh Druids and Bards, called an *"Eisteddfodd"*—which is a public festival event still held annually in Wales. This rite may be amended for any type of group energy work, gatherings and "circle magic" for any number of participants. The ceremonial observation is most effective within a circle of trees and/or stones. Once participants are prepared, procession to the northeast corner of the *Nemeton,* bringing all tools and necessary items with you.

### —OPENING BENEDICTION—

<u>King of the Elves</u>: *May the Source of All Being and Creation grant us favor and protection; and in protection, strength; and in strength, peace;*

*and in peace, understanding; and in understanding comes the True Knowledge of the 'Right Way'; and in the grace of this knowledge may we be granted the will to use it; and in that will, the wisdom to temper the use of knowledge; and in temperance comes mercy; and thru mercy, love; and in love we find the Source of All Being and Creation.*

<u>Faerie Queen</u>: *The recursive spiral path passes through Annwn ('ah-noon') and returns to the love and favor of the Source. Blessed be the All.*

<u>All</u>: Blessed be the Universe.

—GRAND INVOCATION—

<u>King of the Elves</u>: *To bathe in the aethyr of new light and life that swirls about the galaxy. To cleanse away iniquity and mortality so we may join in the harmony of all living beings. Here we stand, beneath the Oaks, beneath the Stones, coming to the place we watched our ancestors go to commune with the Spirit of the Universe.*

<u>Faerie Queen</u>: *The stars shine brightly upon this meeting of our people. The Divine Star shines brightly on us at the hour of our meeting.*

## —ELEMENTAL BENEDICTION—

<u>Faerie Queen</u>: *Let peace ring out through the four quadrants of the Universe. Within our being may we find peace at the center. In the Secret Grove we meet to share peace. Then, as we go about the lives we lead on the 'Surface World,' we radiate the currents of love and peace and attract the same.*

<u>King of the Elves</u>: *Here we stand strong, coming together in answer to the call of our inner vow as Guardians and Keepers of the Earth. Here we stand, side-by-side, heart-to-heart and* [the circle joins hands] *hand-in-hand.* [Release hands.]

<u>Northern Guard</u>: *Guardian of the North, realm and spirits of the Earth Element, 'nature spirits,' Gnomes, Kobold and Drwyds of Falias, hail and welcome to this Nemeton. Extend the currents of peace and stability.*

<u>Eastern Guard</u>: *Guardian of the East, realm and spirits of the Air Element, Ancient and Shinning Ones, Elves and Drwyds of Gorias, hail and welcome to this Nemeton. Extend the currents that enable enlightenment.*

<u>Southern Guard</u>: *Guardian of the South, realm*

*and spirits of Fire, Dragon Priests, fiery sprytes, pict-sidhe and Drwyds of Finias, hail and welcome to this Nemeton. Extend the necessary energy for strengthening the will.*

<u>Western Guard</u>: *Guardian of the West, realm and spirits of the Water Element, ancestral spirits, merfolk, Drwyds of the past and the Otherworld city of Murias, hail and welcome to this Nemeton. Extend the currents of personal well-being and those that enable the insight of wisdom.*

—BARDIC VERSE & STORY—

Traditionally, a gathering of Elven-Faerie, Wizards, Druids and Bards includes recitation of lore and legend to preserve their legacy. It is this very practice that earns the liturgy the name "Eisteddfodd." As an example, these deities and heroes are recognized during specific '*Fire Festivals*' in the modern Celtic Gwyddonic Druid Tradition:

Samhain—Morrigan and Dagda
Winter—Kerridwen and Kernunnos
Imbolc—Bridget and Belenus
Spring—Viviana and Merlyn
Beltane—Belisana and Tarvos

Summer—Rhiannon and Manannan
Lughnassadh—Rosemerta and Lugh
Autumn—Triana and Hellith

—FESTIVAL OBSERVATIONS—

Perform magical operations or ceremonial celebrations that the group has come together to accomplish. You will need to "Cast the Circle" if performing "ritual magic."

—DISMISSAL OF ELEMENTAL SPIRITS—

<u>King of the Elves</u>: *May the Source of All Being and Creation grant us favor and protection; and in protection, strength; and in strength, peace; and in peace, understanding; and in understanding comes the True Knowledge of the 'Right Way'; and in the grace of this knowledge may we be granted the will to use it; and in that will, the wisdom to temper the use of knowledge; and in temperance comes mercy; and thru mercy, love; and in love we find the Source of All Being and Creation.*

<u>Faerie Queen</u>: *Let peace ring out through the four quadrants of the Universe. Within our being may we find peace at the center. In the*

*Secret Grove we meet to share peace. Then, as we go about the lives we lead on the 'Surface World,' we radiate the currents of love and peace and attract the same.*

<u>Western Druid Guard</u>: *Guardian of the West, spirit of the Wave and realm of Sea, we thank thee for thy attendance this day/eve as you witness and remember the ceremony we practice in memory of the rites of our ancestors. May you return again when hence we call. Hail and Farewell. Go in peace.*

<u>Southern Druid Guard</u>: *Guardian of the South, spirit of the Flame and realm of Fire, we thank thee for thy attendance this day/eve as you witness and remember the ceremony we practice in memory of the rites of our ancestors. May you return again when hence we call. Hail and Farewell. Go in peace.*

<u>Eastern Druid Guard</u>: *Guardian of the East, spirit of the Wind and realm of Air, we thank thee for thy attendance this day/eve as you witness and remember the ceremony we practice in memory of the rites of our ancestors. May you return again when hence we call. Hail and Farewell. Go in peace.*

<u>Northern Druid Guard</u>: *Guardian of the North, spirits of Stone and Wood and realm of Earth, we thank thee for thy attendance this day/eve as you witness and remember the ceremony we practice in memory of the rites of our ancestors. May you return again when hence we call. Hail and Farewell. Go in peace.*

—CLOSING BENEDICTION—

<u>King of the Elves</u>: *Before departing from this place, we release the field surrounding this sacred nemeton, grounding the energy of Earth, releasing to the Sky the energies of Air, pushing down the currents of Fire deep into the 'Core of Gaea' and pouring the Waters back into the Sea. So mote it be.*

<u>Faerie Queen</u>: *As we have come in peace, so do we leave in peace. We are the 'Children of the Stars,' beings of light, life and love. In departing, we project and radiate peaceful energy and positive power throughout the Universe, dispersing the energies of light and truth gathered here this day/night. Blessed Be.*

<u>All</u>: *Blessed Be.*

# THE ALARDANA

# alardana festivals and seasonal rites

Many modern neopagan traditions observe some formal annual "calendar" or "Wheel of the Year." Most are inspired by actual "pagan" holidays and festivals based on an ancient observation of "natural cycles" or "seasons," especially those related to agriculture. Observance of cultural festivals is a tradition as old as civilization.

During the early 1900's, a modern standard of eight "*sabbats*" or "grove festivals" was developed by Gerald Gardner (for *Wicca*) and his friend Ross Nichols (for *Druidism*).* The model remains popularly used today, evenly spaced festival observations six-to-eight weeks apart. However, there is some redundancy inherent in the symbolism. For example: the Celtic festival of *Beltane* or May's Eve also correlates with the summer solstice; both are landmarks for the season of growth and maturation.

---

* More details may be found in "*The Witch's Handbook*" by Joshua Free; also included in "*Merlyn's Complete Book of Magick*" anthology.

Beltane is a 'flower festival' marked by an observation of short-lived "may-blossoms" visible in Nature. This begins the 'agricultural summer'. The 'astronomical summer' is observed as the celestial or astrophysical event called the "summer solstice"—which marks a "turning point" in the solar year.

To observe an eightfold cyclic "Wheel of the Year," four *"Fire festivals"*—Beltane, Lughnassadh, Samhain, and Imbolc—are drawn from Celtic lore, supplementing two equinoxes and two solstices each year. This is metaphorically referred to as a 'wheel' that is constantly "turning" the seasons through an annual cycle. Each regional-culture carries its own distinct language-vocabulary or names to define the same kind of seasonal celebrations—such as the Druidic Tradition practiced by many Elven-Faerie folk, which call the solstices and equinoxes the *"Four Albans"*—or "Four Lights"—coinciding with a traditional Celtic "Wheel of the Year."

Origins for popular customs are often taken for granted in mainstream consciousness. For example, the Roman Catholic Church (and "Celtic Church") set their own religious holidays to coincide with dates and relative symbolism of former pre-Christian "pagan" holidays ("holy-days") and festivals. Not only did this aid in smoothing over a conversion of rural agricultural pagan folk —but the Christians were still actively developing their "religion," and incorporated many aspects that do not appear in the Hebrew-Kabbalistic tradition that Jesus actually practiced. Keep in mind—Jesus was a Jew, but he was also shown in scripture as a descendent of the throne of David, and thus a part of an arm of the Dragon Legacy once preserved by the Essene and Gnostic sects. John the Baptist was also an Essene, evident by his use of Essene baptismal rites, borrowed from the pagans, and only used at that time and place by that particular mystic sect. The Church later took ownership of this type of ceremony as well.

The following are standardized dates of the traditional pagan festivals along with the more commonly known observances corresponding to the same times and/or energies. These seasonal Fae-festivals are called *Alardana* (plural) or *Alardan* (singular).

## SEASONAL ALARDANA FESTIVALS

April 30-May 1: *Beltane*, May's Eve, Calen Mai ("First of May"), Tana's Day, Walpurgisnacht and May Day.

June 21 (20-22): *Litha*, summer solstice, Alban Heruin, mid-summer and St. John's Day.

July 31-August 1: *Lughnassadh* ("Marriage of Lugh"), Cornucopia, Calen Awst ("First of August"), Lammas and Lammas Eve.

September 21 (20-23): *Mabon*, autumn equinox, Alban Elved, harvest-fest, Rosh Hashanah and Thanksgiving Day.

October 31-November 1: *Samhain* ("Summer's End"), Shadowfest, Calen Gaeof, Feast of the Dead, All Saint's Day, All Soul's Day and Halloween.

December 21 (20-23): *Yule*, winter solstice, midwinter, Alban Arthuan, Jul, Saturnalia and Christmas.

January 31-February 1: *Imbolc*, Brighid's Day, Calen Geaef, Oimelc,

St. Blaise's Day, Candlemas, Valentine's Day and Groundhog's Day.

<u>March 21 (20-22)</u>: *Ostara*, Eostre, spring equinox, Alban Eiler, Akiti, Sheelah's Day, St. Patrick's Day and Easter.

## SAMHAIN – ALARDAN FESTIVAL

Controversy still exists concerning the time of a proper 'New Year' observantion—but Celtic traditions often begin their annual calendar on Samhain, November's Eve, or October 31. This time period marks an energetic threshold, much like Beltane, when the "veil" between this 'physical world' and the "ALL" is thinnest—but in this instance, the Gate is accessible from the *outside*.

Pagans traditionally observed a "Feast of Ancestors" during "Samhain" (pronounced *sow-en*) meaning "Summer's End" (or '*samhraidhreadh*' in Irish Gaelic) and today we know the remnants of these ancient customs as "Halloween." This includes events like "bobbing for apples," "mask-wearing" and "pumpkin-carving" (reminiscent of the ancient gourd-carved heads).

"Faerie lights" or painted glass orbs with candles inside are suspended from the trees around the *Nemeton*—emitting a cool ultraviolet or cobalt blue light.* Seasonal rites may be performed within a *Nemeton* using the "Eisteddfodd" or "Group Liturgy." They may also be practiced as a solitary, addressing each of the directions in turn.

NORTH: I call thee Northern Spirits of *Lasse*, *Cloch*, *Arbor* and *Elessar*. Join me powers of Leaf, Earth, Tree and Stone, in this celebration of my ancestors. I come to the Sacred Grove this *estevar* ["evening"] to be reunited and guided by their *asha* ["spirit"].

EAST: I call thee Eastern Spirits of *Gaeth*, *Gwai*, *Nel* and *Fin*. Join me, powers of Wand, Sky and Cloud, in this celebration of my ancestors. I come to the Sacred Grove this *estevar* ["evening"] to be reunited and guided by their *asha* ["spirit"].

SOUTH: I call thee Southern Spirits of *Re'Aitai*, *Anar*, *Arva* and *Teine*. Join me, powers of Skyfire, Sun, Flame and Fire, in

---

\* Similar to the '*Pelen Tan*' described in *"The 21 Lessons of Merlyn"* by Douglas Monroe.

this celebration of my ancestors. I come to the Sacred Grove this *estevar* ["evening"] to be reunited and guided by their *asha* ["spirit"].

WEST: I call thee Western Spirits of *Kh'dek*, *Muir*, *Kyela* and *Pehlora*. Join me, powers of Ice, Sea, Water and Love, in this celebration of my ancestors. I come to the Sacred Grove this *estevar* ["evening"] to be reunited and guided by their *asha* ["spirit"].

NORTH: *Glora Duath*. The Sun is overcome by darkness. On this *estevar*, a night outside all other nights, the invisible *evala* ["cloak"] between this world and our ancestor's realm in the Otherworld is thinnest—from their side.

EAST: I call upon the ancestral power of Elvenkind within me. Give me clear knowledge of *Kaloren* [the "Right Path"].

SOUTH: I stand on a threshold between time to witness the death of one year reborn to another. As Keepers of the Earth, Guardians of the Elven *Cor Anar* ["Wheel of the Sun/Year"], I charge the *Duath* ["darkness"] to give way to *alb* ["light"] at Midwinter—the turning point of the Sacred Earth Year.

WEST: In the name of the covenant sworn by Ancient Elvish Wizards that first enticed and communed with spirits of the Otherworld with food offerings, I call out to my ancestors from *Arth Asha* ["spirit world"] to share in this feast with me. Take from this offering the essences you so require.

You may then celebrate your feast. Be sure to leave a portion of it in the northern quadrant as an offering.

NORTH: Behold, I see before me, the Sidhe. They have graced my vision with their presence. They manifested to me, crossed over, transitioned from the Realm of the King. From ancestral mounds they have come this night to celebrate the *Samhain Alardon* ["Festival"] with me.

EAST: Here I stand at *Saeth Duir*, Guardian of the Threshold. I am a portal messenger. Before me the winds rise up to offer their hail and I thank thee spirits of the eastern direction for celebrating with me.

SOUTH: As the ancestral *asha* ["spirit"] depart, I wish peace and love for them on their return to the ancestral plane. I ask only that you leave me with your hereditary guidance that it may be a light to illuminate *Kaloren* ["the Right Way"].

WEST: From the ninth wave I emerge and from nine elements was I created. In nine states of being I channel my power and radiate peace multiplied times nine. By the power of nine may I hope to enjoy the fruits and bounty of another year.

NORTH: Here, I stand in the north on Earth as Guardian of the Threshold. I here seal the Otherworld portal. The ancestral energy and spirits of the dead have passed by this gateway and I bid them peace on their departure. New life comes from death and Nature once more unfolds her mysteries to her initiates. As Keeper of the Earth I shall await the New Light when we shall again meet this winter.

## ALBAN ARTHUANN – ALARDAN FESTIVAL

Long before modern observations of Christmas, ancient cultures celebrated the rebirth of the Sun King at Midwinter on the evening of December 21st—the longest night of the year. In some cultures, the Sun is lured or coaxed back to power with prayers and hymns. Pine trees; evergreen wreaths; symbolism of Oak, Holly and Mistletoe—all originate with pagan Druids. Circular wreaths symbolize the cycle of Life, represented by the annual 'Wheel of the Year'. We have retained customs of "Santa Claus"—that *"jolly ol' elf"*—where we encourage a visit by leaving a "fairy offering" of milk and sweetbreads (cookies).

Use red, green and white candles to illuminate your evening rites, all of which are traditional colors of Druidism and winter solstice. You might even affix the candles to a "Yule Log." The *"Alban Arthuann"* festival —meaning the "Light of Arthur" or "Light of the Bear"—is observed in the evening. After this night, the daytime grows longer and so the Sun is deemed "reborn."

NORTH: I call upon the Spirit of the Forest this eve. Come forth *Aldaron, Herne, Dagda, Kernunnos*—the Green Man and the Antlered One. You do I call upon, the strength of Earth, the elemental forest spirits, on this the darkest of nights.

EAST: *La'Aer, Gaeth, Suk'anar Estevar*. I call upon the power and energy of the Winds and spirits of the Air Element, on this darkest of nights, and a time of new beginnings.

SOUTH: From the south I bind energies of *Re'-Aitai*, Skyfire, *Leollyn*, Great *Anar*, Sun—whose power grows steadily.

WEST: *Muir. Muir. Suk'anar Estevar*. I call upon the power and energy of the tides, activity of splashing water, spirits of the wave and sea, on the darkest night of the year, as Midwinter turns and the Sun's course follows.

NORTH: The turning point is a new birth, one marked by the growing power of the Sun Father, *Leollyn*. As Keeper of the Earth I stand witness to new life coming from death. I stand guard to a gateway of the

Cosmic Law that all things changes.

EAST: The *Cor Anar* ["Wheel of the Solar Year"] turns. I stand waiting encased in a season of hibernation. I am the Morning Star *"el tuile"* ["Spring"] and offer a season of new beginnings and new hope.

SOUTH: *Gaea. Vasta. Gaea. Vasta.* I awaken and arouse the Earth Mother to bare witness to the rebirth of the Sun King. Send forth your energies of creativity and inspiration. Lend us your fiery strength.

WEST: In the *Suk'anar* ["darkest"] *Estevar* ["night"] I call the energy of *Leollyn* ["Sun King"] who is born and reborn here at *Alban Arthuann* [the Winter Solstice] as the "Child" Sun King. From *Numen* ["the west"] I ask to receive the intelligence and wisdom to better use my abilities. Through self-knowledge, I increase my understanding of the Universe.

Light the solstice candles on the Yule Log in the north. If you use evergreen wreaths, light candles in these too.

NORTH: On this *Suk'anar* ["darkest"] *Estevar*

["night"] I call forth the Lord of the Forest by the names: *Aldaron, Ninastre* and *Saelr'ir*, to celebrate and observe the great mysteries of seasonal change and cosmic cycles.

EAST: The time draws near. The Sun King is to be reborn as a child. May all spirits and animals of Nature awaken and know his birth.

Wait in your circle until midnight, continuing your festivities until you wish to close by celebrating the Sun-birth itself. You can continue at midnight, have an all-night vigil until dawn, or you may return just before dawn the following morning.

EAST: *Vasta. Vasta.* Come forth and awaken, power and spirits of *Gaeth* ["wind"], energies of *La'Aer* ["the Air Element"]. Hear me; hear the call of the *Ekahal* ["Elven Wizard"] as I rouse you from hibernation. Rejoice! Rejoice! The Sun King is reborn!

SOUTH: *Vasta. Vasta.* Awaken ye powers and spirits of *Arva* ["flame"], energy of *Teine* ["the Fire Element"]. Hear me; hear the call of the *Ekahal* ["Elven Wizard"] as I rouse you from hibernation. Rejoice! Rejoice! The

Sun King is reborn!

WEST: *Vasta. Vasta.* Awaken, powers and spirits of *Muir* ["the sea"], energy of *Ear Pehlora* ["the Water Element"]. Hear me; hear the call of the *Ekahal* ["Elvish Wizard"] as I rouse you from hibernation. Rejoice! Rejoice! The Sun King is reborn!

NORTH: *Vasta. Vasta.* Come forth and awaken, ye powers and spirits of *Aldaron* ["the forest"], energy of *Lasse* and *Gael* ["leaf and stone"]. Hear me; hear the call of the *Ekahal* ["Elvish Wizard"] as I rouse you from hibernation. Rejoice! Rejoice! The Sun King is reborn!

## IMBOLC – ALARDAN FESTIVAL

*Imbolc* is a Celtic "Candle Festival"—observed with a candle light vigil from the evening of January 31st into the following dawn of February 1st. Even if a vigil is not observed, a candle may be left to burn all night for the protection of the home and family. Meditation on the candle flame has an ability to put you into a trance-hypnotic state. Fire gazing, in general, is known to produce similar calming states. Such activities allow the "inner mind" to be more receptive to visions and prophetic skills may be heightened. Such divination may be performed; most of the subtle energies of this time of year are received at night and during dreams. Imbolc is often dedicated to Brighid (in Celtic Traditions)—elsewhere to Venus and Diana. A 'grain-doll' is sometimes made in the image of such a goddess.

NORTH: I call thee Northern Spirits of *Lasse*, *Cloch*, *Arbor* and *Elessar*. Join me powers of Leaf, Earth, Tree and Stone, in this celebration: a turning of the *Cor Anar* ["Wheel of the Solar Year"] and the strengthening of *Glora Anar* ["the Sun"]. Bless now this *Tuile Alta* ["Springtime Light"] and lend your powers to this candle. [Blessing a candle to be used for the vigil.]

EAST: I call thee Eastern Spirits of *Gaeth*, *Gwai*, *Nel* and *Fin*. Come join me, powers of Wand, Sky, Cloud and Rain, in this celebration of the turning of the *Cor Anar* ["Wheel of the Solar Year"] and the strengthening of *Glora Anar* ["the Sun"]. Bless now this *Tuile Alta* ["Springtime Light"] and lend your powers to this candle.

SOUTH: I call thee Southern Spirits of *Re'Aitai*, *Anar*, *Arva* and *Teine*. Join me, you powers of Skyfire, Sun, Flame and Fire, in this celebration of the turning of the *Cor Anar* ["Wheel of the Solar Year"] and the strengthening of *Glora Anar* ["the Sun"]. Bless now this *Tuile Alta* ["Springtime Light"] and lend your powers to this candle.

WEST: I call thee Western Spirits of *Kh'dek*, *Muir*, *Kyela* and *Pehlora*. Join me powers of Ice, Sea, Love and Water, in this celebration of the turning of the *Cor Anar* ["Wheel of the Solar Year"] and the strengthening of *Glora Anar* ["the Sun"]. Bless now this *Tuile Alta* ["Springtime Light"] and lend your powers to this candle.

NORTH: May all of the Nature spirits and beings, woodland creatures and bipeds, find security, warmth and protection in the *Alta Nwyrve* ["light of the sacred fire"], which I extend as an expression of peace, radiating perfect love throughout the Cosmos.

EAST: From the Radiance within and the new *A'lahn* ["light"] that shines in the *Aiet* ["east"], may all the beings of *G'ea* ["the earth planet"] no longer be subjected to impenetrable *Duath* ["darkness"].

SOUTH: *Tuile F'yonn*, the "Light Season" is soon upon us. As some sprigs of *Tuile* ["the spring season"] and new hope od life appear, the Elven-Faerie Wizards come to commune with the "Elements of Nature," gathered here in this *Kirc* ["sacred circle"] in springtime anticipation.

WEST: *Gaea* breathes the breath of renewal, weaving a web of enchantment that spreads across the land. May the spirits of *Tuile F'yonn* ["the season of light"] bless this land with love and abundance. Energies of *Ear Pehlora* ["the Water Element"] send forth thy spring rains to nurture all life as it strives to grow and mature.

NORTH: Great Lord of the Forest ["*Aldaran*"], come forth and use your ancient magicks to bless the land, making it fertile and green. Bring renewal to all life—every living *Asha* [spirit/soul] of *Arda G'ea* [the earth-planet plane of existence] above and below the Surface World.

EAST: Voice that beckons in the winds of dawn, grant me guidance and inspiration.

SOUTH: Voice echoing strangely through the stillness of the noon's midday heat, speak quietly your secrets.

WEST: Vision that emerges to give form to the voice heard at sunset and in the moonrise, bless me with thy gifts.

Where the liturgy may be amended for use by any number of participants, you will retain the "I" (singular tense) as the following imagery is visualized or imagined.

EAST: I am the wind across the plains and sea. I am a hawk high above the cliffs. I am a raven on a Druid's shoulder.

SOUTH: I am the fire inspiring the minds of sentient spirits. I am the flame that burns in the passion of lovers. I am the beacon of light that permeates throughout the Universe.

WEST: I am a wave crest of the sea. I am the variegated sound coming from the rushing waters. I am a valley lake nestled between two plains.

NORTH: I am a hill of poetry. I am finest of flowers and trees. I am a stone standing watch since the beginning of creation.

Thank and dismiss the energies—wishing them peace as they depart—as with all ceremonies. Then return to your place of dwelling; taking your blessed candle with you. You may consecrate an area of prosperity and protection in the home with it—and if possible, allow it to burn down, extinguishing itself.

## ALBAN EILER – ALARDAN FESTIVAL

The Spring Equinox goes by many names, including Ostara, Eostre, Ostera, Eastre and finally Easter. *Alban Eiler* is often observed on the dawn of March 21st. These kinds of festivals once ran three or more days in duration—observed perhaps from the 20th to the 23rd. In ancient Babylon, the New Year festival of Akiti and first month of Nissanu began on this day—observed by the whole urban population for ten entire days.

If ground and weather conditions allow, you might make this a seed-planting ceremony. You may even use pots if outdoors is not an appropriate choice. Both the spring and autumn equinox mark observable times of equality (or balance) between daytime and nighttime—or else, the Sun and Moon.

NORTH: I call upon the Spirit of the Forest at the dawn of the *Tuile F'yonn* ["Spring Season of Light"]. Come forth *Aldaron, Herne, Kernunnos*—you who come when I call on the strength and power of the Earth Element and forest energy. Merge your stream with this Grove, this Sacred *Nemeton*. Come and celebrate the Springtime Equinox.

EAST: *La'Aer, Gaeth, Tuile F'yonn*. I call upon the power of the winds and energies of the Air Element on the dawn of the Spring Season of Light, this time of new beginnings. Be here now to witness and remember my ceremony.

SOUTH: From the south, I bind the power of *re'-aitai*, the skyfire, and *Glora Anar*, the strength of the Sun that has returned. The air of the east blows to the south and it is warmed. Come now and celebrate *Alban Eiler* ["the spring equinox"].

WEST: *Muir. Ear Pehlora.* Energy and power of the waters and sea, I call thee here now to share in an ancient observation of the equinox, the festival of balance between day and night.

NORTH: As all beings yield to the new *A'Lahn Tuile* ["light of the spring season"], I plant new seed and call upon powers of the "Elements of Nature" to bless and encourage its growth.

As part of a seed-planting ceremony, you might choose an appropriate flower/herb for each direction, or use "pots." If necessary, you may even visualize the seed-planting process.

EAST: At the eastern ward I plant new seeds of psychological well-being.

SOUTH: At the southern ward I plant new seeds of spiritual well-being.

WEST: At the western ward I plant new seeds of emotional well-being.

NORTH: At the northern ward I plant new seeds of physical well-being.

EAST: Spiritual powers of *La'Aer* ["the Air Element"], caretakers of all flowers and trees—take and scatter my seeds among fertile soil. Bless and keep safe all new life that begins in *Tuile* ["the spring"].

SOUTH: *Sier Arva* ["sacred fire"], searing flame, spirits of the same, ensure that the Radiance of *E'Graine Glora Anar*, bright sphere of the Sun above, shines down to nourish these seeds with life-giving warmth and light.

WEST: Spirits of *Ear Pehlora* ["the Water Element"], the gentle rains and *Muir*, Element of Sea, come forth and bless this new life with your lustral waters, moisture and nourishing rains.

NORTH: I place the life of all new seed in the hands of *Gaea* and the invisible caretakers of the Green World of Nature. O Spirits of *Talamh* ["the Earth Element"] accept the seeds of new life into your folds.

EAST: Spirits of the *Duile* ["fey elements"], you have been called to this *Kirc* ["sacred circle"] *Nemeton* to observe, recognize and remember the ancient tradition observed.

SOUTH: Today, I call upon and receive the strength of the heavens, warming light from the Sun, to invoke the splendor of the Element of Fire...

WEST: Depth of the Sea and radiance of the Moon...

NORTH: Stability of Earth and firmness of stone...

EAST: Speed of lightning and swiftness of Wind.

NORTH: The cyclic phases of *Gaea* and the laws of the Green World of Nature are marked and observed with the rotation of the *Cor Anar*. The Great Wheel turns again.

### BELTEINE – ALARDAN FESTIVAL

The *Belteine* or *Beltane* festival is named such after the "Fires of Bel" or "Belinos"— most likely a remnant of Bel Marduk or "Lord Marduk," the patron god of Babylon, known elsewhere in the mutation of "Baal." It was actual on the dawn of an ancient Belteine when the *Tuatha d'Anu* arrived in Ireland and set fire to their own ships. The most frequently cited tradition of May Day is, of course, the "May Pole"—erected as a symbol of the "World Tree" and then usually danced around while weaving ribbons.

By some calenders, Beltane was observed in mid-April, when 'May Blossoms' are first visible. "May Day" is, of course, May 1st, though the festival often begins the night before—on May's Eve—with construction of two large bonfires built side-by-side, which are consecrated to Bel, then set aflame. Ancient Celts marched cattle in procession between these two flames as they led them out to pasture for the year. Some evening observances may be held, however this following rite is typically observed at noon.

NORTH: I greet you *Alardon*, Spirit of the Grove, Spirit of the Green World. I call forth northern energies of *Lasse*, *Cloch*, *Talamh* and *Arbor*. Join me, powers of Leaf, Stone, Earth and Tree as we celebrate the mysteries of creation at the height of *F'yonn Thuile* [the "season of light"].

EAST: I greet you *Gwai*, Spirit of the Sky. I call thee forth from the east to celebrate the forthcoming *Laer Reudh* ["summer season"] marked by the Fires of Bel. Energies of *Gaeth*, *Fin* and *Nel*—spirits and powers of the Wind, Air and Cloud—grant me thy inspiration and guidance.

SOUTH: Spirits of *Laer Reudh Arva* ["the summertime flame"], now is the time to emerge, come forth and shine brightly. Power of the southern spirits, open your *Evala Duir* ["hidden door"] of mysteries. Join me in celebration of summer's anticipation.

WEST: I hail from the *Kirc*, this sacred *Nemeton*. Hear me, *Kh'dek*, *Muir* and *Ear Pehlora*. Spirits and powers of the last receding Ice, the warming Sea and the Element of Water, join me now, this *Beltaine Alardon* ["Beltane festival"].

All ritual candles should be lit from a central flame or bonfire consecrated to "*Bel*." In the event that candles are not appropriate, you may substitute lanterns or torches. Color themes for Beltane are red, yellow-gold and green.

NORTH: Lady of the Earth, Lord of the Greenwood, Spirits of the Grove, nature spirits and woodland creatures, come now to this *Nemeton* and share in the spiritual fire of *Bel*.

EAST: May this sacred time of *Belteine* rekindle the heart and inflame the spirit of all living things in creation.

SOUTH: As a Keeper of the Earth, Guardian of the Elemental Mysteries, I stand to observe a turning of the *Cor Anar* ["Solar Wheel of the Year"]. *Glora Llew Anar* ["spirit of the Sun"] I await the day of your solstice apex and keep watch as you grow in strength each day.

WEST: *F'yonn Thuile*, the Light of Spring is coming to a close, making way for *Laer Reudh* ["the summer season"]. Today begins *Twythron Thrimidge* ["the month of May"] sacred to the *Dwyr* ["great Oak Tree"].

NORTH: Elements of Nature, Forces of the Green World, heed my call this day. Open up your oaken door and reveal thy mysteries to me, a servant of the Earth Planet and follower of the Elven Ways. I seek the wisdom of creation and abilities to channel all energy currents of the cosmos. And to the same, I am a keeper and guardian for all my days.

At this juncture, you may consider a recitation of the "*Cad Goddeu,*" or "Battle of the Trees." In any case, retain the "I" in these following statements as they are visualized.

NORTH: I am a *Cloch* ["stone"] hidden in the *Saeth* ["unseen folds"] of *Talamh* ["the Earth"] and in *Milana Abrahor Terrest* ["an ancient emerald forest"].

EAST: I am a yellow *Alta* ["ray of light"] of *Glora Anar* ["blessed Sun"].

SOUTH: I am a *Dwyr Arva* ["flaming door"] concealing the secret laws of creation.

WEST: I am a blue-crested wave under *Isil El'orel* ["the Moon"] concealing mysteries of the purple depths of *Muir* ["the sea"].

You may observe the tradition of the Maypole and feast. After the feast and any activities, the convocation concludes.

NORTH: *Laer Reudh* ["the summer season"] comes upon us quickly. It graces now by every bud, blossom and leaf.

EAST: On the dawn of the morrow, the Earth shall be set upon her "Golden Path" toward the season of maturity.

SOUTH: The great *Cor Anar* ["Solar Wheel of the Year"] continues to turn once more, now bringing us every nearer to the "Red Season," but ever turning.

WEST: And may peace radiate throughout the universe.

## ALBAN HERUIN – ALARDAN FESTIVAL

The "Summer Solstice" marks a time of mystical significance throughout ancient Æurope. For as long as we can remember, Elves, Druids, Mystics and Wizards have performed Midsummer Rites. In Western Europe, these were frequently vigils held at sacred stone "*Kircs,*" like Stonehenge on the Salisbury Plains in England. Thousands of "*Kirc*" remains are scattered throughout the mainlands. While the festival may begin the day before, this rite begins approximately ten minutes before the dawn of the solstice itself—usually June 22nd. It is the longest day of the year.

NORTH: I call upon the Spirit of the Forest in the twilight of the great Elven-Ffayrie Rade between the worlds, before the dawn of *Laer Reudh*, the "Red Season" of summer maturity. Come forth *Alardon*, *Herne*, *Kernunnos*, the Green Man—those entities that arrive when I call on the strength and energy of the Earth Element and the Enchanted Forest. Share your energies with this Sacred Grove.

EAST: The threshold is drawing near. The forthcoming power of *Glora Anar* ["the Sun King"] peaks to bless the lands of *G'ea* in celestial marriage. May the spirits of *La'Aer* come forth to share in this great observation of the season.

SOUTH: Hark! On the horizon awaits the Sun on the longest day of *Cor Anar*. *Arva*, *Teine*. I summon the spirits of flame and the power of high noon's heat to come forth on the occasion of this *Alban Heruin* ["summer solstice"].

WEST: The dawn of *Glora Anar* ["the Sun"] is upon us/me, only moments away. I call ye spirits and energies of *Muir* ["the sea"] and

*Duile Ear Pehlora* ["Element of Water"] to come forth and share celebration of this Summer Solstice with me.

NORTH: *Glora-Anar*. Mighty Sun Father, share your power with me now in your time of greatness. I am a Keeper of the northern ward, and Guardian of the Earth while you sleep.

EAST: *Glora-Anar*. Mighty Sun Father, share your power with me now in your time of greatness. I am the Keeper of the eastern ward, guarding the direction of your birth.

SOUTH: *Glora-Anar*. Mighty Sun Father, share your power with me now in your time of greatness. I am a Keeper of the southern ward, Guardian of the mid-day peak during your travels through the sky.

WEST: *Glora-Anar*. Mighty Sun Father, share your power with me now in your time of greatness. I am the Keeper of the western ward, guarding the station of your daily retirement.

Moments before dawn, the leader says: *"Mighty Sun, be here now."*

Then the rite continues after dawn has peaked.

EAST: As Guardian of the East, I hail that the Sun is upon us.

SOUTH: Hail to the Great Sun King Llewollyn rising in the sky.

WEST: Hail to the Great Sun King that warms the oceans and the sea.

NORTH: Hail to the Great Sun King, the supreme light bearer parading through Enchanted Forests.

EAST: I smell the fragrance of the summer flowers.

SOUTH: I am warmed by the spirit burning within all life.

WEST: I am blessed by the love in all life flowing throughout the Green World of Nature on Earth and in the Universe.

NORTH: May the love and energies called here for the *Alban Heruin Alardon* ["festival of Summer Solstice"] be radiated as perfect peace by all spirits present for this occasion.

## LUGHNASSADH – ALARDAN FESTIVAL

The ancient Celtic festival of *Lughnassadh*—pronounced "*loo-nass-ah*"—is observed on August 1st (or on the eve of the same) and means literally: "The Wedding of Lugh"—a solar deity in the Celtic pantheon derived from the *Tuatha d'Anu*. This marriage of the "sun and sky" with the "land" marked the first harvest festival and start of the harvest cycle—which runs through the autumn season until the eve of *Samhain*.

The *Lughnassadh* festival is a time for blessing an forthcoming harvest and offering the first grains cut as a sacrifice back to the Earth and its spirits. For this ceremony, bring a sufficient supply of fresh bread and wine to the *Nemeton*. Traditional lore also suggests the custom of "*Lammas Towers*"—a competition to see who can build a larger bonfire that stands upright for the longest period of time. The rite is aligned to the sunset/dusk (autumn) threshold.

NORTH: I call thee Northern Spirits of *Lasse*, *Cloch*, *Arbor* and *Elessar*. Join me, powers of Leaf, Earth, Tree and Stone, in this observation of another turning of the *Cor Anar* ["Wheel of the Solar Year"]. Bless now this harvest time. Darkness appears distantly in the north as the Wheel continues to spin.

EAST: I call thee Eastern Spirits of *Gaeth*, *Gwai*, *Nel* and *Fin*. Come and join me, powers of Wand, Sky, Cloud and Rain, in this observation of another turning of the *Cor Anar* ["Wheel of the Solar Year"]. Bless now this harvest time as we must prepare for an inevitable winter.

SOUTH: I call thee Southern Spirits of *Re'Aitai*, *Anar*, *Arva* and *Teine*. Join me, powers of Skyfire, Sun, Flame and Fire, in this observation of another turning of the *Cor Anar* ["Wheel of the Solar Year"]. Bless now this harvest time, spirits of *Dan Harad* ["the southern direction"].

WEST: I call thee Western Spirits of *Kh'dek*, *Muir*, *Kyela* and *Pehlora*. Join me, powers of Ice, Sea, Water and Love, in this observation of another turning of the *Cor Anar* ["Wheel of the Solar Year"]. Bless and observe this harvest, and the wedding feast of Lugh here observed by the ["name of the Grove"].

NORTH: This *Calen* ["day"]/*Estevar* ["night"] I gather in the sacred *Nemeton* of the Grove to observe the Ancient Elven-Ffayrie festival of *Lughnassadh*. Here we mark the beginning of the harvest season. Here we celebrate the wedding feast of *Lugh*, hence all friendly spirits are invited.

KING OF THE ELVES: In order to eat, whether plant to us, or meat to other-kin, something must die. This is the law of Nature: that no energy shall be created or destroyed, only finite in number, changed and altered through processes. The energy may be exhausted if not renewed, so it must be maintained responsibly.

FAERIE QUEEN: When we eat of the sacred harvest, or the hunt, honor must be given to the sources of that energy that we take into ourselves. By this we honor the being that is the source of the food and its life, and the Source of All Being and Creation who is the source of the essence of life that is within the being and food, and life must be maintained responsibly.

Go to the central workspace and take up the

bread, holding it outward and asking for benediction from the spirits present.

NORTH: Elemental powers of the ancient and sacred *Terrestai* ["the everlasting or eternal forest of the Universe"], spirits of Nature, Earth and Stone, you that arrives when I call on the power of *Tuath* ["the north"], spirits of the fields and harvest, spirit of the grain, I thank thee for your precious wheat, fruits and roots. All who share in the feast of this bread will also share in your eternal blessings of bounty and prosperity.

Return to the central workplace and replace the bread with the wine, taking it up and extending it outward as you ask the spirits for benediction.

WEST: *Duile Muir Ear Pehlora*, Elemental powers of Water and Sea, powers of of *Muin* ["the vine"], I thank thee spirits for your precious drink, as we might drain blood, so do we drain the wine from the grape in our harvest. Spirit of the wine, bless this drink and all who share it.

NORTH: All ye friendly spirits gathered at

this Sacred Grove, this most holy *mandala* ["magic circle"], may you share in this feast in honor of the first harvest, the covenant of agricultural tradition, shared in offering for the wedding celebration of *Lugh* to the land.

Here you may celebrate the feast, sharing the "bread and wine." Remember to bring a portion of this feast in offering, placed at the northwest, saying: *"May the spirits of Nature accept this sacrifice, sowed and reaped using the knowledge granted by the covenant between the Earth Children and the Ancient and Shinning Ones."* Each participant may wish to offer a portion of their feast in a similar fashion before completing the rite.

NORTH: Nature is the greatest of all teachers. The Keepers of the Earth share these mysteries of creation as Guardians of the *Cor Anar* ["solar year"]. We come each turn in seasonal celebration eight times annually. Here in the sacred place of ancients I gather Elemental energies to weave a place worthy of such celebration.

EAST: Split wide the fruit of the seeds that

have been sown and open the door to the ancient mysteries. As we share in the harvest, we share the wisdom of the cosmic law and the universal energy that makes all growth and life possible.

SOUTH: Source of All Being and Creation, kindle the formless and sacred *Nwyvre* ["divine fire"] of *gnosis*, inspiration and true knowledge in my head. Share in the eternal *Alta* ["light"] that is inextinguishable and an ageless source of true wisdom.

WEST: Great Spirit of the Western Winds that blow over the sea, energies and beings radiating from the sunset's beauty and evening twilight, come and share these blessings from the "elixir of wisdom" before departing this *Nemeton* in peace and perfect love.

NORTH: Deep within the secret folds of the forest lies the source of Elven knowledge—the Sylvan Library. Open your "Books of Light" and grant us true knowledge. Share with me your ineffable wisdom as I share with you the ancient covenant woven into this mystic elemental temple, consecrated here and now to observe *Lughnassadh*. Partake in our harvest and accept the sacrifice of ["name of the group or Grove"].

EAST: Change is ever upon us as the great seasons cycle. We must prepare for this each year, the changes. So, the harvest must be brought in to sustain life in a season of death. Spirits of *La'Aer* ["the Air Element"], *Giet Romen Gaeth*, powers of the Eastern Wind, come and share in the energy of this "Magick Sphere," bless and receive this combined sacrifice—a labor of love between the Earth and its children. Depart in peace to spread the winds of fortune on all harvests in the world.

SOUTH: Behold the passion of *Laer Reudh Anar*, the "Summer Sun" that dims as the *Duath* ["dark"] half of the year turns. Its lifeforce received in growing things which we receive in our nourishment. But change is always present in Nature, and we must observe and live in harmony with these changes, as the cycle of life, death and renewal turn once more. Mark well and remember this observation of the ancient covenant, departing in perfect peace and perfect love, and returning to this place again when we celebrate the turning of the Wheel.

## ALBAN ELVED – ALARDAN FESTIVAL

An ancient name for this festival may be translated literally as *"Light of Elves."* This ceremony is traditionally practiced as a part of a "Thanksgiving Feast" in honor of the harvest, and as an observation of the "Autumn Equinox," the rite is part of a festival that peaks on September 21st.

As with *Alban Eiler* (the Spring Equinox), forces of light and dark—or day and night—are in balance with one another. With light giving way to darkness, the season of death is soon setting in. Harvest festivals are often observed at dusk. [This liturgy incorporates a "consecrated feast" and creation of a *"satchet"* ("pouch") containing "Mistletoe."]

NORTH: This *Kus'anar* ["evening/twilight"] I do call upon *Aldaron* ["spirit of the forest"], *Herne*, *Dagdha*, *Kernunnos*, and Green Man's spirit. You are summoned to gather here for this *Alban Elved* ["Autumn Equinox"] observance. I call to you that answer when I summon the solidity of Stone and powers of Earth. Come forth now and be present to celebrate these ancient mysteries.

EAST: This *Kus'anar* ["evening/twilight"] I do call upon *La'Aer* ["Element of Air"]. You are summoned to gather here for this *Alban Elved* ["Autumn Equinox"] observance. I call to you that answer when I summon the intensity of Wind and powers of Sky. Come forth and be present to celebrate these ancient mysteries.

SOUTH: This *Kus'anar* ["evening/twilight"] I do call upon the Southern Ward, radiant energies of *Re'Aitai*, Skyfire and the final rays of strength extended from *Glora Anar* ["the Great Sun King"] now fading. You are summoned to gather here to observe this *Alban Elved* ["Autumn Equinox"]. I call to you that answer when I summon up the strength of Flame and powers of Fire. Come forth and be present to celebrate these ancient mysteries.

WEST: This *Kus'anar* ["evening/twilight"] I

do call upon *Muir, Ear Pehlora*, and the spirits of the place where the Sun sets. Hear the summons to gather here and observe this *Alban Elved* ["Autumn Equinox"] ceremony. I call to the spirits that answer when I summon forth the fluidity of Sea and powers of Wave and Water. Come forth. Be present to celebrate these ancient mysteries.

NORTH: At this time of year, those who live by the ways of nature—magical folk and woodland creatures—all make haste to ready their harvest before the frost. Now we take rest and offer thanksgiving to the spirits of the harvest and of Earth.

EAST: I come to acknowledge and observe the ancient ways; ancient ways that I maintain and uphold whenever I remember and keep the Elven Tradition. I adhere to the secret and sacred covenant between *G'ea* ["spirit of the Earth planet"] and the Keepers of the Earth, her mysteries and traditions.

SOUTH: I stand in recognition to observe the ever turning *Cor Anar* ["wheel of the Solar Year"] at the time of equinox, the balance of light and dark. The harvest season is midway and all preparations must be made to survive the winter. The last scythe shall fall at *Samhain*. So, we come to extend our thanks for the food that will sustain all life through the dark months.

WEST: From *Gwaith* ["shadows"] of *D'yonn Reudh* ["the autumn season"] comes the cycle of *Hrive D'yonn* ["winter"] and death. *Gaea* ["the Earth Mother"] shall never perish so long as her faithful Elven-Ffayrie Guardians are there to serve and protect her. This is our responsibility.

NORTH: As the harvest is taken in, winter plans are made. I guard a season of inner exploration as the Earth ["*Gaea*"] and Sun ["*Glora Anar*"] hibernate in winter ["*Hrive D'yonn*"].

EAST: The secrets of the *Cor Anar* ["Wheel of the Sun"] are symbolic and well-hidden, but they offer to us the keys of self-realization. I will stand guard and wait for the season of new growth and beginnings as *Gaea* ["the Earth Mother"] and the Sun ["*Glora Anar*"] awaken in *Tuile F'yonn* ["spring season"].

SOUTH: The ancient power of the Elves, Faerie, Druids and Wizards shall never perish if the traditions do not cease to be observed. This is our responsibility. At this time of year, the Keepers of the Earth gather in the secret forest to reaffirm their Oath to Nature and remember the ancient covenant as it recedes in slumber. Let Earth rest easy in her season of hibernation, knowing that her Guardians are ever-present in stewardship while she sleeps. I stand guard a wait for the season of fullness and maturity as *Glora Anar* ["the Sun"] warms in *Laer Reudh* ["the summer"].

WEST: It is the equinox. At this time *Isil El'orel* ["the Moon"] sits in balance with *Glora Anar*. I stand guard and mark the ebb and flow of Autumn [*D'yonn Reudh*] and ask all the forces of nature to bless our food, our spirits and our path.

At this juncture, members prepare an amulet-bag containing the herb, mistletoe. It is consecrated in ceremony (using the consecration rites), then later hidden away for future use. At the northern quarter, each participant blesses their amulet-bag.

NORTH: May this sacred herb of the ancient —the Mistletoe—be consecrated for the future use of *Sylvan Druidecht* ["Elven Forest Magick"]. May its contents activate all herbal remedies and potions that I prepare during the forthcoming year with goodness and love. May this amulet bag itself be charged as a symbol to guard away misfortune in my life and home.

Invite friendly spirits gathered at your *Nemeton* to join in the essence of the feast you have prepared, making certain to leave a formal offering in the north—inviting the energies or entities present to partake in the bounty before thanking and dismissing them.

# the annual "cor anar"
## de'ea canayen istari elandra

### DYONN—"The Dark Season"

Narbeleth: Winterfilthe (October)
2nd – Alardenna: Festival of Spirit Guides
31st – Samhain: Night of Ancestors

Yestare: Newmoth (November)
1st – New Year's Day
11th – Lunatasidhe: Eve of Faerie

Rithon: Foreyule (December)
21st – Alban Arthuann: Winter Solstice
24th – Holly Day
25th – Oak Day

Narvinye: Afteryule (January)
18th – Danuhal: Festival of D'Anu

### FYONN—"The Light Season"

Ninui: Solmath (February)
1st – Imbolc: Festival of Brighid
15th – Hal Pan: Festival of Pan

Sulime: Rethe (March)
21st – Alban Eiler: Spring Equinox

Virith: Astron (April)
7th – Yn Offeryn: Day of Sidhe Offerings
23rd – Hal Kernunnos: Green Man Festival

Lothron: Thrimidge (May)
1st – Beltane: The Fires of Bel

## REUDH—"The Red Season"

Norui: Forlithe (June)
21st – Lithe/Alban Heruin: Summer Solstice
23rd – Elnassadh: Wedding Festival of the
King and Queen of Faerie

Cerveth: Afterlithe (July)

Uruime: Wedmath (August)
1st – Lughnassadh: Wedding Feast of Lugh

Iavaneth: Holymath (September)
21st – Alban Elved: Autumn Equinox

The calendar is partitioned to correspond with 'months' that a modern reader is most familiar with. Lore suggests that when plotted on a fixed calendar, transition from one month to another occurs on the 21st; not the 30th etc. Some versions align with lunar phases, beginning a month with a "full" moon, a "new moon" or even the "sixth day of the moon."

*Would*

*you*

*like*

*to*

*know*

*more*

*???*

*Participate in the Mardukite Academy from anywhere in the Universe.*

*Master Edition Anthologies and Academy Grade Lecture Volumes now available in hardcover!*

## CLASSICS OF MARDUKITE MESOPOTAMIA
## REVISED HARDCOVER 2-VOLUME SET

### SUMERIAN RELIGION

*Introducing the Anunnaki Gods
of Mesopotamian Neopaganism*

*Mardukite Liber-50*
by Joshua Free

### BABYLONIAN MYTH & MAGIC

*Spiritual Traditions and Mysticism
in Mesopotamian Anunnaki Religion*

*Mardukite Liber-51+E*
by Joshua Free

**SYSTEMOLOGY BASICS HARDCOVER SET**

### THE POWER OF ZU
*Applying Mardukite Zuism and
Systemology to Everyday Life
Systemology Liber-S1-Z*
based on a lecture series
by Joshua Free

### THE WAY INTO THE FUTURE
*A Handbook for the New Human
Systemology Liber-S1-W*
collected works mini-anthology
by Joshua Free

**THE METAPHYSICS OF STRANGER THINGS**

*Telekinesis, Telepathy & Systemology*

by Joshua Free

in hardcover and paperback

**ANUNNAKI TAROT**

*The Babylonian Oracle (Second Edition)*

*Mardukite Liber-T*

by Joshua Free

A guidebook featuring the Archetypes of the Major Arcana in Ancient Mesopotamia.

*First time in hardcover!*

**THE
WAY OF THE
WIZARD**

*Utilitarian
Systemology*

*A New Ethic for
Metahumans*

by Joshua Free

in hardcover
and
paperback

**IMAGINOMICON**

*Approaching
Gateways to Higher
Universes
(A New Grimoire
for the
Human Spirit)*

*Systemology
Liber-3D*

based on the lectures
by Joshua Free for
Mardukite Academy
in revised hardcover

# SYSTEMOLOGY
## The Pathway to Self-Honesty

**GO FURTHER AND BE**

CRYSTAL CLEAR

JOSHUA FREE

# CRYSTAL CLEAR

## (Handbook for Seekers)

*Mardukite Systemology Liber-2B*
by Joshua Free

Take control of your destiny
and chart the first steps
toward your own spiritual evolution.
Realize new potentials of the
Human Condition with
a Self-guiding handbook for
Self-Processing toward
Self-Actualization
in Self-Honesty using actual
techniques and training
provided for the coveted
"Mardukite Systemology Grade-III
Self-Defragmentation Course Program"
—once only available
directly and privately from
the underground Systemology Society.

Discover the amazing power behind the
applied spiritual technology
used for counseling and advisement in
the tradition of Mardukite Zuism.

19 95  JOSHUA FREE  20 20

PUBLISHED BY THE **JOSHUA FREE** IMPRINT REPRESENTING

**The Mardukite Academy of Systemology**

THE JOSHUA FREE IMPRINT
JFI PUBLICATIONS

MARDUKITE
ZUISM

**mardukite.com**